CHAMPIONSHIP TRACK & FIELD

Volume 2: FIELD EVENTS

edited by
JOHN RANDOLPH

Leisure Press
P.O. Box 3
West Point, N.Y. 10996

A publication of Leisure Press.
P.O. Box 3, West Point, N.Y. 10996
Copyright © 1982 Leisure Press
All rights reserved. Printed in the U.S.A.

ISBN 0-918438-15-2
Library of Congress Number 79-92134

Front Cover Photo: Don Gosney
Back Cover Photo: David Madison
Cover Design by Diana J. Goodin
Except for Chapters 1, 5, and 26, all materials used by permission
ATHLETIC JOURNAL.

CONTENTS

Part 2: The Horizontal Jumps

Long Jump

Triple Jump

Part 3:The Vertical Jumps

High Jump

Pole Vault

PREFACE

In selecting these articles from the pages of *The Athletic Journal,* I have attempted to provide a collection of materials that go beyond the boundaries of the typical text written for the track and field coach.

Instead, *Track and Field by the Experts* is a two-volume series designed to provide the coach with a wide array of *practical* knowledge and tools to enable him or her to help the athlete succeed.

A thorough background in technique studies is provided by the many "frame-by-frame" pictures of champions performing in each event. A number of different training philosophies and methods are also included. Here I have attempted to represent the many and varied ways that can produce winning results for the athlete.

Finally, by including a broad cross section of training ideas I have endeavored to encourage innovation and experimentation on the part of the coach. This is done in the belief that variety and ingenuity are integral parts of the total process of challenging and motivating athletes towards the realization of long range goals.

Track and Field by the Experts offers the coach and athlete many ingredients that can result in success. The selection and blend of these ingredients into a recipe for winning track and field is the challenge that awaits the reader.

John Randolph

Part 1
The
Throws

1
SHOT PUT TECHNIQUES

Jack Harvey
University of Michigan

THE BASIC (CONVENTIONAL) SHOT PUT FORM

STARTING POSITION
(The following description is for a right-handed putter)

- Shot resting on the base of the fingers.
- Shot placed on the neck just in front of the ear and below the jawbone.
- Right foot pointed to the rear of the circle, or rotated slightly in the direction of the throw and weight on the ball of the foot.
- Eyes directly in back of circle focused about fifteen feet from circle.
- Most putters start from the upright position with both legs extended, then drop slowly to the following position.
- Right leg flexed as close to 90 degrees as possible.
- Shot directly over right foot or slightly further back.
- Left leg flexed and pointed in straight line parallel with line of movement.
- Left arm semiflexed across front of body to maintain balance and the upper body torqued to the right.
- Right elbow about 45 degrees from shoulder plane, in comfortably close to body.

Emphasis

- Putter must be comfortable. **Relaxation** is the key.
- Once the shot is in motion, you must keep it in motion and increase its velocity (gradual acceleration).
- Use the left arm to keep the upper body in a torqued position.

GLIDE

- Smooth controlled start for maximum efficiency and best form.
- Accelerate in a straight line with as little side or up and down motion as possible.
- A slight upward rise usually begins here with first acceleration.
- Kick back left leg and push off right leg simultaneously.
- The landing should find the individual facing the same direction from which he came.
- The only conscious effort that should be made in addition to speed and relaxation should be the turning of the right foot counterclockwise, while keeping the upper body torqued to the right.

Emphasis

- Gradual relaxed acceleration.
- Work with legs ahead of upper body.
- Turn right foot into the throw while keeping upper body torqued to the right.
- Attempt to draw the right leg under the center of gravity.
- Maintain torque and squared shoulders.
- Stress the concept of active lower body and passive upper body.
- Left leg should be planted simultaneously with right. The toe pointed into the direction of the throw. Toe of left foot should be in line with heel of right.
- Hips are partially open.

POWER

- Eyes still on focus point.
- The right leg remains flexed, ready for the lift.
- Left foot is planted in center or just left of center of toe board and is used as a lever to convert lateral acceleration into vertical acceleration (similar to high jump).
- Left foot should be parallel to line of flight.
- Right foot should be perpendicular, or better yet, turned into the direction of the put.
- Left leg is partially flexed, ready for lift.
- The hips will be open in the direction of the put while the upper body is still in a torqued position.
- The back has begun to lift upward.
- This closed position is held as long as possible to give a quicker second acceleration stage.

Emphasis

- Try to keep the flight of the shot in a straight line from the back of the circle through the release.
- Think of up and over instead of around and out.
- Left leg bends, then straightens (as in high jump or LJ take off leg)
- Start to uncoil your torqued upper body.
- Rotation is stopped by left leg, hip, and arm.
- Follow flight as long as possible with eyes.
- Keep elbow behind shot.
- Once center position is reached, then think of **explosion**
- To experience explosion, you must drill and throw many times. USUALLY, explosion is only experienced in a meet situation under great desire when you are fully in control of your form. A sort of "controlled

Right leg push. The right leg should be bent at just about right angles so maximum speed and strength can be had. It straightens pushing the body, still closed, toward the line of put.

The body turn. The upper body opens as the leg gets its full extension. As the upper body starts turning and the hips move forward, the weight is shifted on to the fully extended left leg which vaults the body up into the put.

Chest lift. The left arm swings around bringing the chest up into the put. Be sure to keep the eyes on the put and the chest up.

FOREARM AND WRIST

The forearm comes straight out from the elbow and follows out a 41-degree maximum angle. It is not a hook or round-house punch type. The hand, turned inward at this point, should rotate so the fingers point slightly upward. The shot should be as far up in the fingers as possible so as to give more whip and snap because the fulcrum (wrist) is further away from the ball. The index finger should be the last one to leave the shot.

FOLLOW-THROUGH AND REVERSE

This is simply what happens after the shot has received the acceleration from the center of the circle through the right leg, hip, shoulder, chest, and arm. It should be natural and used only to aid proper form and prevent fouling.

Emphasis

- Delay as long as possible.
- Should be natural and not a practice phase.
- If you are having trouble with your reverse, trace it back to your position in the center of the circle.

THE DISCUS-STYLE SPIN IN THE SHOT PUT

STARTING POSITION

- Same as that for the discus: feet slightly wider than shoulder width apart, left arm level with shoulders, legs slightly bent as if "sitting in a chair."
- Shot is carried the same as the conventional form but the elbow is slightly higher.
- Slight wind-up is used to increase the distance through which the shot will move.

FIRST TURN

- Pivot on the left foot but keep the left arm up and the shoulder square to the ground.
- Drive forward with the left leg and the right knee.
- The right leg should land near the center of the circle to begin the final 180° turn.
- The shot and body weight are centered over the right foot.

13

- Both legs remain flexed.
- The left leg makes contact as soon as possible to stop the rotation and begin the conversion of linear to vertical.

FINAL HALFTURN

- Position is very similar to the power position in the conventional shot put form.
- Rotation is stopped with the left side of the body (i.e., arm and leg).
- Drive is from the right leg to the left.
- The left leg becomes very important not only to stop the rotation, but also to convert the horizontal to vertical.

FOLLOW-THROUGH REVERSE

- Same as the conventional shot put form.

CONCEPTS TO EMPHASIZE IN THE DISCUS-STYLE SPIN

- Active lower body and passive upper body.
- Keeping the shoulder square to the ground and leading with the left arm up.
- Good combination of linear drive and rotation out of the back of the circle.
- Timing between landing of the right foot and left leg. The left leg **must** snap down quickly to stop the rotation.
- Double leg lift at the front of the circle **after** the leg has stopped the rotation.
- Use of the left arm as a guide throughout the form and finally as a stopper of upper body rotation.
- If the proper amount of rotation and linear force has been **applied** and **converted,** then the reverse will be no different than a properly executed conventional throw.

Strength is important for the double man, because without power even the well-coordinated all-around athlete will not be able to achieve his maximum potential.

2

TRAINING FOR THE SHOT PUT AND DISCUS DOUBLES

Charles Thomas,
Texas A. and M. University

In order to develop a double champion (shot put and discus), a coach must have a big, strong athlete, one who has natural all-around athletic ability, excellent coordination, and considerable power. These are the qualities possessed by Randy Matson, best weight double man in the history of track and field. He has put shot 70 feet, 7 inches, and tossed the discus 201 feet, 5½ inches.

Randy's natural all-around athletic ability, in addition to hard work, made it possible for him to achieve his fine records by the time he was a junior in college. At 6 feet, 6½ inches, and weighing 260 pounds, Randy has the coordinated power and speed of a man much smaller. He made all-state in high school basketball and all-district in football, once ran 10.2 out of the blocks in the 100-yard dash, and as a freshman broke the existing 60-yard dash indoor world record for boys in his weight division. This season he went out for basketball after a two-year layoff and has already made the starting team at our school. Many basketball critics said it would be almost impossible for him to make the varsity team since he had never played college basketball.

Well-rounded ability is important for a weight man and this can be further illustrated by two other good double men who attended our school. In 1962, Danny Roberts threw 60 feet, 7 inches, and 185 feet. He was 6 feet, 3 inches, weighed 240 pounds, and had high jumped 6 feet, pole vaulted 11 feet, 6 inches, and ran a 50.5 440 in high school. Darrow Hooper placed second in

17

the 1952 Olympics in the shot put and had a double of 57 feet, 3 inches and 170 feet, very good in 1952. Darrow was an outstanding football player and still holds several school field goal kicking records.

Strength is important for the double man, because without power even the well-coordinated all-around athlete will not be able to achieve his maximum potential.

Matson's training schedule consists of weight training eleven months of the year. He does all types of exercises to develop his whole body, such as wrist and ankle developer exercises,but his main concentration is on power. He works with weights three days per week for eleven months, taking only one month off for complete rest. His exercises consist of the bench press, full and one-half squats, inclined dumbbell press, and jump squats.

We feel it is important for the weight man to have a full three to four months of general body conditioning to develop strength, endurance, and improve coordination before actual shot and discus practice begins. A boy can become discouraged very quickly if he starts practice too early, before his body is in good condition. During the months of September, October, November and December we do not throw the shot and discus. The workouts during this early season consist of running up and down the football stands, which develops the legs and helps develop fast foot and leg action. Randy will sprint up and then down the stands as fast as he can go.

Danny Roberts played a great deal of handball, which is good to improve speed and coordination. Randy does a considerable amount of fast running on the track. After warming up, he never does any slow running. His running consists of short dashes from 30 to 60 yards from the blocks. His longer runs consist of several fast repeat 150 and 220 yards. Occasionally, he will sprint 300 to 330 yards and even ran through a 440 at three- quarters to five-eighths effort, Before Randy starts practice with the shot and discus, he is in good physical condition. He works hard in the weight room during early season training. He is playing basketball this season, hoping it will give him a better background for the spring. During basketball season his weight training will be cut down to two days per week.

After practice with the shot and discus is started, the first two or three weeks are devoted to getting the feel of putting the shot and throwing the discus from a stand. During January and February, Randy throws in the ring, working on form and technique and not trying for distance.

Due to the indoor season, we are forced to begin the shot workouts a little early. Practice with both the shot and discus is conducted almost every day, five days per week, during the months of January and February. In March, Randy usually begins to practice throwing four days per week and in April three days per week. In May and June the practice sessions are cut to two days per week.

Matson throwing the shot: illustrations 1-6.

Matson throwing the shot: illustrations 7-12.

Matson throwing the discus: illustration 1-6.

Matson throwing the discus: illustrations 7-12.

Randy always puts the shot before moving over to practice discus. Usually, he will run several fast 150 yard wind sprints between the shot and discus workouts. During the main competition season he does not practice with the shot and discus on the same day that he works in the weight room. A typical workout week in April and May would consist of weight training on Sunday, Tuesday, and Thursday, practice in the ring with the shot and discus on Monday and Wednesday, complete rest on Friday, and meet competition on Saturday.

After the season has started and his technique is good, Randy never throws easy for form. He always throws hard (both shot and discus) in practice. He uses an 18-pound shot when warming up and will occasionally throw it for distance. Early in the season Randy will throw hard (shot) about ten to fifteen times, trying to have all throws over 62 feet. When his technique is not just right, he will work on parts while still throwing hard, but concentrating on the technique on which he is working. Matson's theory in the shot put circle is that the position is more important than speed across the ring. He takes a very slow, deliberate movement in his glide across the ring, but comes up fast with a great deal of power from the center of the ring through the release. He wants to have correct position and form before coming up to release the shot.

Randy has one technique which is different from that of other shot putters who use the O'Brien style. Putters using the O'Brien form shift or glide out of the back of the circle, shift their weight far across before the right foot leaves the back of the circle, and the heel of the right foot leaves the ground last. Randy keeps his shoulders well back and shifts only the weight of his left leg and hips, and the toes of his right foot leave the ground last at the back of the circle. This movement is shown in Illustration 3. We think it tends to slow him down in his shift but gives him a stronger position in the shoulders and hips. With Matson's height and long legs, he would have trouble with fouling and losing power if he concentrated on speed instead of position in the glide across the ring.

Randy has a very fast arm with tremendous explosive power. While he is a little slower from the push-off to the center of the ring, we believe he is faster than other shot putters from the position where he drives up through to the release, and here is where the speed and his explosive power get the great distances. When he gets off a good throw, he spins and makes a complete circle after the release, which helps maintain balance and prevent fouling. Illustration 12 shows the start of the complete turn.

In the discus, Randy's fast arm is more evident. His form in the discus is not as good as it should be and he needs considerable work in this area. During the latter part of April, May and June, Randy throws quite a bit less in practice than he does before his technique is good. For example, in the shot put he will only put four to six times a workout twice a week when everything is working right. During this time all puts will be in the neighborhood of 66 feet. In other words, when he can hit 65 and 66 feet on his first or second put, then he will only put five or six times. He likes to leave the ring knowing his form is correct and while he is feeling good. If he has dificulty throwing 65 feet early, then he puts longer, until the mistakes are corrected and 65 and 66 feet come rather easily.

However, Matson works and throws longer with the discus, because his discus form is not as good as his shot put form. Sometimes he will throw the discus for an hour to an hour and a half without stopping. He worked very little with the discus his freshman year because he was concentrating on making the Olympic team in the shot. So Randy has really had only one year's work with the discus, and for this reason, we believe he still has considerable room for improvement.

Following is a week's workout schedule one week prior to Matson's great double of 70 feet, 7 inches, and 199 feet, 7½ inches in the Southwest Conference meet on May 8, 1965.

Sunday - One and one-half hours hard workout in the weight room.

Monday - Short practice with the shot and discus. Six good throws with each (45 minutes).

Tuesday - Light workout on weights (30 minutes).

Wednesday - Short practice about 30 to 40 minutes. Five good throws each with the shot and discus.

Thursday - Complete rest.

Friday - Complete rest.

Saturday - Set a world record of 70 feet, 7 inches, and the west Conference discus record of 199 feet, 7½ inches.

3

HIGH SCHOOL RECORD HOLDER'S TRAINING PROGRAM

Vern Wolfe
Phoenix High School, Phoenix, Arizona

When Dallas Long reported for track at North Phoenix High School, most of the members of the teaching staff did not expect him to become the potential weight prospect he is today. Because he stood 5 feet, 11 inches and weighed 185 pounds, we felt the weights would be his best events. The O'Brien technique was introduced to him and he acquired a great interest in the shot and discus from a senior teammate, John Harper, who had been dominating the state for three years. Harper's marks were 56 feet, 7¼ inches and 160 feet, ½ inch without the benefit of a weight training program.

From the accompanying progression chart, we hope to show the value of an organized system of weight training for the shot and discus events. Only a few routine lifts will be listed to show how Dallas' strength has increased as a result of his schedule. We added his progression in the shot, discus, and 100-yard dash as well as his growth in height and weight.

Year	Ht.	Wt.	Shot 12 lb.	Discus	100-Yd.	Full Squats With Barbell On Shoulders	Standing Two-Arm Military Press	Two-Arm Bench Press
9	71"	185	42'	117'	13.6	90 lbs.	90 lbs.	90 lbs.
10	73"	200	56' 8 3/8"	137'	12.8	125 lbs.	125 lbs.	125 lbs.
11	74"	210	61' 5"	158'	11.2	200 lbs.	200 lbs.	200 lbs.
12	76"	245			11.2	350 lbs.	275 lbs.	350 lbs.

Table 3-1. Dallas Long's progression during his high school years.

Photos #1-9 show a put by Dallas of 65 feet, 3-3/8 inches made in exhibition. One week later Long broke the national high school record in competition.

Dallas was not put on his schedule until he finished his freshman year. Weight training must be given most of the credit for Long's unusual improvement in the shot and discus, because improved technique and maturity alone could not produce such marks. As a sophomore, Dallas broke Harper's state shot record as well as our school record, and began to show promise with the discus. To this day his interest in the discus is not too great and, as a result, his form leaves much to be desired. After having a great year as a sophomore, Dallas reached the turning point in his career as a weight man. He resumed his weight program with new interest and desire. When he reported to school in September of his junior year, he was a much stronger, better coordinated boy, eager to win a starting berth as tackle on the varsity football team. Long received all-state honors which gave every indication that he would become a fine football player as well as a shot putter. After football season, he had a good year in track and became the first junior to hit over 60 feet, posting 61 feet, 5 inches and 158 feet with the discus.

This past summer Dallas increased his strength tremendously and in July he put the twelve-pound shot 65 feet, 2 inches, worked the sixteen-pound to 55 feet, 7 inches, and let the discus fly in the neighborhood of 180 feet. This improvement led him to pass up football in his senior year. In spite of the pressure put on Dallas to play, he stuck to his decision, hoping that it would make him a great weight man rather than a good 60 footer.

In many respects Dallas' improvement in strength after his junior year was fantastic. We wonder just what he might have done had he specialized for four years. As a junior, Dallas had his form work between 56 feet and 58 feet for the shot and 145 feet to 150 feet in the discus. At present he has been ranging from 61 feet to 65 feet and 160 feet to 175 feet. Every indication shows that, barring injuries, Dallas should come close to his goals set for the year: 70 feet for the shot and 190 feet for the discuss.

Here is the weight schedule Dallas and our other weight men use. The starting poundages will have to be left up to the coach and to each boy. Encourage the boy not to start too heavy.

LEGS

- Full squats with the barbell on the shoulders. Three sets. Ten to 12 repeats.
- Half-squats with the barbell on the shoulders. Three sets. Ten to 12 repeats.
- Jump squats with the barbell on the shoulders. Three sets. Ten to 12 repeats.
- Straddle hops with the barbell on the shoulders. Three sets. Ten to 15 repeats.
- Calf raises with the barbell on the shoulders. Three sets. Twelve to 15 repeats.

MID-SECTION

- Sit-ups. Three sets. Ten to 15 repeats. Weight may be added behind the neck.
- Leg raises. Three sets. Fifteen to 20 repeats. Weight may be added by using iron boots.
- One-arm side bends with dumbbells. Three sets. Fifteen to 20 repeats.
- One-arm dead lift with dumbbells. Three sets. Ten to twelve repeats.

FINGERS

- Finger flips off a wall. Three sets. Ten to 15 repeats.
- Finger push-ups off the floor. Three sets. Ten to 15 repeats.

TWO-ARM EXERCISES

- *Standing.* a. Two-arm barbell military press. Three sets. Three to five repeats. b. Two-arm dumbbell press. Three sets. Six to eight c. Two-arm barbell snatch. Three sets. Two to four repeats. d. Two-arm barbell clean and jerk. Three sets. Two to four repeats. e. Two-arm barbell curl. Three sets. Three to five repeats.
- *Prone Position.* a. Two-arm barbell prone press on a bench. Three sets. Ten to twelve repeats. An incline board may also be used. b. Two-arm dumbbell prone press on a bench. Three sets. Eight to 10 repeats. c. Two-arm barbell pull-over. Three sets. Six to eight repeats.
- *Seated.* a. Two-arm barbell press on a bench. Three sets. Four to six repeats. b. Two-arm dumbbell press on a bench. Three sets. Four to six repeats.

ONE-ARM EXERCISES

- *Standing.* a. One-arm barbell or dumbbell military press. Three sets. Six to eight repeats. b. One-arm dumbbell clean and jerk. Three sets. Four to six repeats.
- *Seated.* One-arm dumbbell press on a bench. Three sets. Six to eight repeats.

DISCUS

- Lateral raises with dumbbells on a bench. Three sets. Twelve to 15 repeats.
- Flying motion with dumbbells on a bench. Three sets. Twelve to 15 repeats.
- Standing lateral raises with dumbbells. Three sets. Fifteen repeats.
- Arm swings with a wall pulley. Three sets. Fifteen to twenty repeats.

It is necessary to spend hours with young weight boys, explaining lifting techniques, starting poundages, breathing, when to lift, how to organize the program, length of the workout, how and when to increase weight, and other things conducive to good weight training. It is recommended that our boys join the local health clubs during the summer months in order to get expert instruction in the use of their facilities.

We lift three days a week off-season with at least one day's rest between. A boy may select one or two exercises from the main groups, the arms, legs, fingers, and mid-section, giving him the eight to ten exercises for the day's work. We allow a boy to choose the type of lifting he prefers. That is he may lift by muscle groups or by alternating his exercises from one area to another. If he were to alternate his exercises, a typical day's workout might be as follows:

- Two arm barbell snatch. Three sets. Seventy, 80 or 90 pounds. Seven to 10 repeats.
- Half-squats. Three sets. One hundred, 110 or 120 pounds. Ten to 12 repeats.
- Two-arm barbell prone press on a bench. Three sets. Eighty, 90 or 100 pounds. Ten to 12 repeats.
- Sit-ups. Three sets, Ten to 15 repeats.
- Calf raises with a barbell on the shoulders. Three sets. One hundred, 110 or 120 pounds. Twelve to 15 repeats.
- Finger push-ups off the floor. Three sets. Ten to 15 repeats.
- One-arm barbell or dumbbell military press. Three sets. Twenty, 30 or 40 pounds. Six to 8 repeats.
- One-arm dead lifts with dumbbells. Three sets. Fifty, 55 or 60 pounds. Ten to 12 repeats.

After three weeks, the workout can be changed to include other exercises from the main groups in order to avoid monotony.

The length of the workouts will range between one and a half to two hours. We like to increase our weights by 5 or 10 pounds between sets. Normal progression for three exercise periods a week would call for increasing the starting poundages 5 to 10 pounds. Naturally, this progression will vary greatly in each boy. The same poundages should be used for at least three workouts. Rest between sets and exercises will also vary, but generally two or three minutes between sets and two to four minutes between exercises will be adequate. For better progress and a more systematized schedule, have the boy keep a chart and record his exercises and the weight he lifts. All lifting techniques are very important to the beginner and this information can be obtained from any good book on weight training.

Our boys are asked not to rush the program. A point that is stressed, and the one we believe is responsible for our success, is that the exercise be fast and explosive rather than slow and deliberate. In our opinion, this type of action gives the kind of strength necessary for the shot and discus competitor. Adequate bulk should be developed, but unless it is flexible and explosive we would rather not have it.

Dallas follows a diet similar to that of thousands of other American boys. Of course, his training is strenuous and special attention to proper food is important. He has been taking a food supplement - minerals and vitamins, plus a high vegetable protein diet.

Three weeks before the first meet we lighten the weight program in order to sharpen the reflexes and explosive strength. The first week we may eliminate one set on Monday and Wednesday, and do the full three sets on Saturday. The second week the boys often do only two sets on Monday and eliminate the Wednesday lifting entirely. Saturday they do all three sets. The week prior to the first meet they lift only on Monday and Saturday, and continue this procedure for the remainder of the season. A coach must watch his boy and regulate this tapering off as he sees fit. On the day after a meet, the boys lift all three sets hard in order to maintain the strength reached during off-season lifting.

Our weight training program has produced visible proof of its merit. Karl Johnstone, a junior discus thrower, hit 175 feet this year, and has been lifting only two years. We believe track coaches throughout the world are convinced of the value of weight training in track and field. This is a new field to many of us but one which track coaches should be eager to learn and adapt to their track programs. New ideas continue to make track and field records go by the boards and move high school marks closer to college and world records.

We should add that our shot and discus training program includes much more than working with the weights. Our boys do many short dashes, 100, 220 and 440-yard runs to keep agility high. Tumbling, rope climbing, bar work, and hand standing all have a place in our schedule.

To venture into the O'Brien technique would be repetitious since many qualified authorities have covered the subject adequately. We do stress balance, continuous rhythm, position, use of the entire body, and explosive action. It is not the technique that Dallas used or his strength which has made him the weight man he is today. Many other factors enter the picture. Dallas has a fine personality, lives by Christian ideals, is a strong B student, and possesses the burning desire to become the world's top weight man. Jim Brewer, his teammate last year, was a great inspiration to Dallas. Brewer proved that hard work, perfect training habits, sacrifices, and confidence will produce exceptional athletic achievements. Dallas Long possesses every quality necessary to become a champion and we are happy to be associated with such a fine boy.

4

IMPROVING THE PERFORMANCE OF THE EXPERIENCED SHOT PUTTER

Patrick G. Wyatt
Sweet Home High School, Buffalo, New York

One of the most frustrating and discouraging situations that a track coach can experience is to have an experienced shot putter fail to improve his distance from one year to the next. There are many reasons why this can occur, and it will be the purpose of this article to pinpoint many of these problems and offer suggestions for their correction.

The first problem we call *too-much-too-soon.* In twenty-one years of experience as a coach and competitor, we have found this factor to have contributed more to the failure of athletes to improve their distance than any we have observed. There is a natural tendency for the young, inexperienced competitor to grab the shot the first day of practice and try to put it into orbit. This tendency must be curbed or many times it will lead to early season hand and finger injury. Almost without exception, the young putter's fingers and wrist are not sufficiently conditioned to withstand the tremendous strain of full effort putting resulting in finger and wrist injury which can retard progress for an entire season.

Late pre-season and early season training should emphasize conditioning of the fingers and wrist. It is our opinion that this part of training a shot putter is most often neglected.

One conditioning exercise for this area we have found successful is called the finger flip. The athlete stands with his right arm extended over his head holding the shot at the base of his fingers with his wrist flexed and his fingers pointed toward his face. Then with as little arm movement as possible, using mainly the wrist and the fingers, he tosses the shot in the air, catching it on the fingers as it comes down. This action is repeated for 8 to 20 repetitions and as many sets as the atheletes's fingers and wrist can take. In pre-season, a light shot should be used, and as the athlete's strength increases, heavier shots should be introduced.

The second exercise, which is effective for finger and wrist conditioning, is called wall flips. The athlete stands with his hands on the wall and his fingers pointed inward. His body should be at an angle to the wall in order to place a large portion of his weight on his fingers. Resistance can be increased by placing his feet a greater distance from the wall to place more weight on his fingers. The athlete should continue this exercise until his wrist and fingers become fatigued.

The second pitfall, although not as obvious as the first, can be just as damaging. The athlete makes great improvement very early, often in the second or third practice session. This appears to be a good result, but later without the proper foundation of conditioning and technique training, he invariably falls into bad form habits, and his initial improvement is followed by a drastic decrease in distance. This leads the performer to the conclusion that he must try harder to improve and with this increase in effort his technical problems increase, adding to his frustration and contributing to additional loss of distance. More times than not, at this point the short season is just about over and the athlete's improvement is doubtful. We call this phenomenon early peaking.

Another procedure which can be used to cut down on finger injuries and early peaking is to start pactice, using lighter shot such as an 8- or 9-pound shot in the case of the high school athlete. If an 8-pound shot is not available, a knotted towel will suffice. The athlete will find it easier to hit the proper position and execute the actions correctly due to the decreased resistance. Decreased resistance places much less strain on the fingers and wrist and allows them time to develop and condition to the point necessary. In addition, since he cannot tell how far he is going to throw the regulation shot, the athlete can forget distance and concentrate on execution. With emphasis on execution, he will groove himself more quickly in the proper technique, making his future improvement with the regulation weight more rapid. This early training also tends to sharpen the athlete's desire to put the regulation weight, thus hastening his progress in technique development. We have found that when the transition is made from the lighter shot to the regulation weight, not only is the transfer of learning greater but much of the explosive speed is retained.

Another method which can be an effective early training tool is placing an indoor shot up against a brick wall at a distance of about 10 to 15 feet. At first this idea seems strange until it is examined closely. By putting into the

One of the most frustrating situations facing a track coach is to have an experienced shot putter who fails to improve his distance from one year to the next.

wall, the desire for distance is eliminated (it can only go 15 feet), allowing the athlete to concentrate on technique while putting at maximum effort. Many more puts can be taken because the shot travels such a short distance and can be retrieved easily and quickly. In addition, by observing the height at which the shot hits on the wall, the coach can tell if the athlete is getting proper lift from his legs and back. The correct point of impact can be computed easily by taking the height of release of the shot by the athlete and adding it to the distance of the toe board from the wall, taking the total, subtracting 2 feet, and measuring that distance up the wall. Of course, this would be a theoretically perfect angle of trajectory for the 60-foot put. As the athlete's distance decreases, so would his angle of release and the point of impact of the shot on the wall, say 24 inches for every corresponding 5 feet decrease in distance. Therefore, a 60-foot putter with a 7-foot high release point, and the circle 15 feet from the wall, should put to a point on the wall of approximately 20 feet in height. A 55-foot shot putter at the same release height should hit about 18 feet up the wall. A 50-foot shot putter should hit about 16 feet, etc.

Problem: Unable to break through a plateau. We discovered that improvement in the shot put follows what can be called a plateau pattern. An athlete will improve in stages. As an example, a shot putter is throwing 48 to 50 feet consistently for two weeks, and one day he breaks through and throws 53 or 54 feet. Now he becomes consistent at 51 to 53 feet with a top of 54 feet. This phenomenon has been experienced by most throwers and becomes a frustrating experience. If not understood, it can produce anxiety and apathy which can result in a decrease in distance and consistency.

Solution: First, the athlete must understand the plateau phase and realize he must continue his training to break through to a new level. There are some techniques and methods that can be used to combat this problem.

Use of a heavier shot can be of value in drop-in standing throws. The athlete stands at the toe board with both feet together and his back in the direction of the throw.

Then he steps back, slightly to his left, and drops in a deep crouch position which is an exagerrated power position in the center of the circle. From this position he executes the basic mechanics of a standing put. The coach should emphasize a low position and full effort puts. This resistive work has a tendency to make the regulation shot feel lighter, develops strength in the muscles involved in putting, and helps develop the effective use of a lower putting or power position.

The second technique is to make use of different exercises and methods in the weight training regime. Some exercises we have found successful are:

• **Standing Lateral Raiser with Dumbbells.** Emphasis is placed on complete movement from the sides to directly overhead.

- **Standing Dumbbell Curls and Presses.** Both should be done simultaneously and in an explosive manner during the resistance part of the exercises.
- **Power Snatches.** These should be done with very little if any foot movement, emphasis on speed.
- **Standing French Curls with a Barbell.** Hand spacing should be close. The athlete should make sure his arms are warmed up thoroughly before he begins these exercises.
- **One Arm Dumbbell Push Press.** This is done with explosive movement in mind and at near maximum weight.
- **Barbell Push Outs.** The bar is held at chest height, pushed out at about a 45 degree angle, and pulled back after full extension of the arms. The nature of the movement is explosive.

The third method of breaking through is called blitz putting. For this putting at least three shots and three helpers are needed to retrieve the shots. The blitzing putter begins with a full effort put across the circle. Then this is followed immediately by another put at full effort. It is continued with each put being taken with no rest between and as rapidly as possible, until the putter is completely fatigued. A blitz program should be done only at the end of the workout day. Twice or three times a week are plenty for this type of stress training. Using it more frequently may retard progress.

When dealing with individuals, it should be remembered that what works for one may not work for another.

At least one day a week should be devoted to film study and technique discussion. During this film study time, no physical work should be done. This should be a complete rest day. It has been our experience that this day of study and reflection can do a great deal to solve many of the mental problems faced by a young competitor. It is a false assumption that if hard work does not bring improvement, harder work will. Many times the athlete will try so hard that the very force of his effort will have negative results by developing new technique faults, anxiety will grow and cause him to tie up, and worst of all, the athlete will become discouraged and lose heart.

By way of illustration, we would like to relate an experience that happened to us while coaching weight men at a local high school. One of the athletes we were coaching was a very intense young man. In early season, his improvement from 38 feet to 48 feet was very gratifying but at this distance he hit a plateau which put him three feet shy of his major competitors. The harder he worked, the more frustrated and disheartened he became, resulting in a disastrous decrease in distance. It was at this point we instituted a program which involved film study and discussions of technique three times a week and putting only in meets and after competition. The results were positive. The athlete seemed to regain his composure, his distance almost immediately improved to his former level, and in the conference championship meet he improved to 50 feet which placed him second with a new school record. Although this case is extreme, the use of films and discussions did a great deal to hasten the improvement and development of this shot putter by relieving his anxiety, giving him a chance to rest, and his body an opportunity to recover and gain in strength.

When dealing with individuals, what works for one may not work for another. A coach must always experiment and try to find what training devices are right for each putter. Some of these brainstorms may appear to be disastrous, but from each, new insights are found which will eventually lead to the proper course of action. Always be optimistic and remember, one word of encouragement is better than 1,000 words of criticism.

5

BASIC DISCUS TECHNIQUES

Jack Harvey
University of Michigan

GRIP

- Comfortable finger spread.
- Good grip with 1st knuckle on index finger over rim.

STANCE

- Foot placement should be slightly wider than shoulder width.
- Weight is on the balls of the feet.
- Legs are slightly flexed as if the thrower were sitting on a chair.
- Back is straight and head is level.

PRELIMINARY SWINGS

- Relaxes thrower and places the thrower in a torqued position for beginning of throw (1 or 2 swings only).
- Body weight is shifted with each swing.

TRANSITION

- Begin the acceleration of the discus in a smooth and controlled manner.
- This acceleration begins before the discus has reached its farthest position to the right.
- Body weight is transferred smoothly from the right to the left.
- From this point onward, the lower body leads and the upper body follows.

MOVEMENT TO THE MIDDLE OF THE CIRCLE

- Maintain body position and use the lower body and body weight to continue acceleration.
- The left leg is compressed and the right knee becomes the driving force. (Similar to a sprinters start.)
- Head and shoulders remain level and the left arm becomes a lead.

LANDING IN THE CENTER OF THE CIRCLE

- Good position is the primary objective.
- Should land in a loaded position. (Bent right leg and torqued upper body.)
- Head, shoulders, and discus arm level.
- Left foot must be brought down as quickly as possible to stop further rotation and, thereby, maintain torque.
- Body weight must be over the right leg to insure the right leg drive into the throw.

FINAL DRIVE

- Begin final drive *after* front foot has reached proper position.
- Initial drive is begun by turning right knee then right hip as the right leg is being extended.
- Body weight is shifted onto and into front leg.
- Upper body comes from its torqued position as a reaction to the stop in rotation and forward drive generated by the lower body.
- Head is up and into the angle of release, shoulders level, discus arm at or near shoulder height.

FOLLOW THROUGH AND REVERSE

- Should be as natural as possible and if throw is executed properly, there should be a minimum amount of rotation and forward drive left.
- Concentration should be on following the discus with the eyes and avoid fouling.

DISCUS THROWING DRILLS

- Stand throws with towel.
- Stand throws.
- Step into stand throw.
- Run into stand throw.
- Jump into stand throw.
- Tape discus to hand for practice on 1st turn; move to center of circle then stop and check position.

WEIGHT EXERCISES FOR DISCUS

- Bench Press wide grip.
- Squats.
- Inclined Bench Press.
- Inclined Bench flies and flat bench flies.
- Cleans.
- Snatches.
- Curls.
- Torso Twist.
- Step-ups.
- Sit-ups twist with weight.
- Press.

*Pictured are: Scott Eriksson: 1981 Big Ten Champion, 173' 3½'', Sophomore, Engineering major; and Penny Neer: 1981 Women's Big Ten Champion, 172', 5th AIAW, first woman Track All-American at the University of Michigan, Senior, Computer Science major.

When leaving the hand, the discus should roll off the index finger last and in a clockwise rotation.

6

DISCUS THROWING TECHNIQUE

Leo Lang
Los Altos, California, High School

In this article, we shall describe the basic discus training program that has been used at Los Altos High School for the past dozen years. Under this program the following throwers have been developed: Scott Overton (1972) California State Champion and pending national record holder with a throw of 204 feet, 3 inches; Bob Stoecker (1962) former state and national record holder with a throw of 195 feet, 4 inches. Other outstanding discus throwers we have had at Los Altos include Jay Pushkin 187 feet, 9 inches; Chuck Smart 183 feet, 6 inches; Steve Davis 181 feet; Max Leetzow 177 feet, 6 inches; Randy Schneider 176 feet; and Randy Patterson 175 feet, 7 inches. We have had numerous other discus throwers in the high 160's and low 170's.

Before going into the basic technique description of discus throwing, we must say that we regard the discus event as only one-sixteenth of our total track program. We have dedicated athletes and coaches who see the value in developing a winning and successful track and field program which includes emphasizing the importance of being well balanced in all sixteen events in a track meet. Our discus throwers are typical of the caliber of young men we have in track, inasmuch as they are willing to put in three hours of hard work daily to achieve success. In its fourteen-year history, the school has won well over 100 dual meets while losing only three.

Recognizing that there is more than one form to use in throwing the discus, an attempt will be made to explain some of the fundamentals we use in coaching this exciting event. To be sure, each boy differs in size, speed strength, coordination, and mental temperament. However, all of our discus throwers use basically the same technique and appear similar in their form. We are not attempting to explain fully each phase of the throw in this brief article, but to stress the key points, as we see them, in modern discus technique. In our estimation, the most important thing in coaching the weight events is for the coach to communicate his observations on form faults to the athlete in language he understands. For example, a coach can tell an athlete something over and over and then one day he will cite an example, or use different words, and the boy immediately grasps the idea.

FUNDAMENTALS

Grip. The throwing hand should be placed on the discus so that the first joints of the first three fingers are hooked over its edge. The fingers should be spread to give balance and stability to the implement. The thumb and little finger should be in a relaxed position. If a boy has a small hand, the index and second finger can be moved closer together. When leaving the hand, the discus must roll off the index finger last and in a clockwise rotation. A good drill for beginners is to roll the discus along the ground like a wheel a few times to get the feeling of it coming off the index finger in a clockwise rotation. The discus should be cocked during the backswing in order to get more whip out of the wrist.

Stance and Preliminary Swings. We have our beginners throw from a stand for several days in order to master smooth flight and proper delivery action off the fingers. After a week or so, the turn is started.

The thrower begins with his back toward the direction of the throw. His feet should be approximately shoulder width, his back foot should be up against the ring, and his left foot should be a couple inches from the ring. Preliminary swings vary from one to three. The main thing is to get the thrower to relax and to prepare mentally for the throw. Our discus throwers are taught to literally explode into the throw. Setting goals and believing they can be reached are our best aids in developing track stars.

For example, goals are set for our throwers to reach from a standing throw. Overton could throw 180 feet from a stand. Of course, each boy progresses at his own level of ability, but we try to get everyone using the full turn as soon as they are capable of controlling the implement.

The Turn. When he is ready to spin, the thrower should bring the discus as far back as possible, but still maintain balance. His left heel will lift off the surface and the thrower's weight will be shifted to the one-quarter bent right leg. His body is twisted at the waist, the thrower takes a deep breath, and expands his lung cage. The spin is started by transferring all of the body weight to the ball of the left foot. It is vitally important that all of the thrower's weight is momentarily on the ball and the toes of his left foot. We emphasize pretending that the left foot is on a scale, and as the thrower drives off, he should try and make the dial of the scale show as much weight as possible.

Next, the thrower should swing his right leg around, leading with the foot and knee. As soon as the right foot reaches the 10 o'clock position, it should be snapped down into a strong throwing position near the center of the ring.

46

The left foot comes off the surface in a jumping-driving motion and is brought past the right foot quickly and fairly close to the right leg on its way to the post position at the front of the ring. We feel the left foot should land slightly in the *bucket*. This allows the hips to get into the throw mode fully. Another form tip here is to get the left foot down almost simultaneously with the landing of the right foot.

Throwing Position. After completing the turn and landing in a strong throwing position (with controlled momentum), the thrower should start a violent thrust with his right leg. In fact, the split second the right foot touches the surface the throw should be started. A good teaching technique at this phase of the throw is to think of the ring as a hot stove lid and get into the throw (fast). The moment the thrower's left foot lands at the front of the ring, it also lifts and braces against the thrust of the right drive leg. Our throwers are told to try and release the discus before the right leg comes off the surface. It is impossible, but they do get into the throw with a solid base of power. The action that takes place during this phase of the throw is so very fast it is imperative to work on many drills in order to perfect that part of the throw. Some drills we use are: 1) Throw low and drive right on out of the ring. 2) Run into the ring, jump into the throwing position, and then jump out after the throw. 3) Squeeze the legs together at the moment of release getting *tall*.

The thrower's head and eyes should be kept fairly well on a level plane during the entire throw. When he starts his upward thrust, then his head, chest, and shoulders should all come up high and out. His left arm should be pulled back and down slightly at the moment of release. We believe it is important to lift off the surface about three to six inches with both feet a split second after the discus leaves the hand.

Upon landing after the discus leaves the hand, all of the thrower's weight should land on his right foot. We emphasize the idea of getting the discus moving at an incredibly fast rate of speed at the moment of release and coming down hard on the right foot to brake the forward momentum.

Drills emphasizing from slow to fast acceleration are used and the throw is also broken down into parts with a wide variety of techniques. We think the best method of developing champion discus throwers is to instill into the throwers the desire to throw several thousand times in practice and work on fundamentals, using drills as mentioned previously. We try to instill in our throwers the desire to be the very best they can be. Anything an athlete imagines vividly, desires ardently, and believes in sincerely, with proper work or training, can be achieved. We are thinking of a 250-foot high school discus throw. All our track athletes think big and believe in themselves. In the past twelve years Los Altos has had five state discus champions and hardly a year goes by that one of our track athletes does not place in the California State Meet.

The thrower's head and eyes should be kept fairly well on a level plane throughout the entire throw.

Discus Throwing Technique

Illustration 1 shows Scott Overton turning the corner and starting to gain momentum. Notice how he is driving off his left foot and leaning into the turn.

As shown in Illustration 2, his right foot is almost perfect as he starts to land in a strong throwing position.

The discus is being held back and Overton's right hip is tucked under for maximum hip thrust.

Illustration 4 shows Overton's left foot is slow in coming down. At this point both feet should be down almost at the same time. The discus is being held well back indicating good technique.

Overton is in a strong throwing position with the discus back behind his driving leg (Illustration 5). The discus is facing the ring flat which is a key to a smooth flight angle.

Illustrations 6 and 7 show why Overton is the greatest high school discus thrower of all time. He snaps the right side of his body against a rigid left side and goes up and after the throw vertically. His left arm is starting to pull around and back keeping him in balance.

As shown in Illustration 7, Overton's left toe should be a little more open or pointing forward. Notice how he holds his left leg down and straight. He gets terrific snap at this split second of the throw.

Overton has left the ring too early at this point (Illustration 8). His left leg should still be in contact with the ring. This throw could have gone well over 200 feet if the post leg had been held down just a little longer.

Excellent vertical lift and follow-through are shown in Illustration 9. Overton's head is up and his upper body is in perfect balance.

As shown in Illustration 10, Overton's right arm will help carry him around as he balances and pulls back with his left arm.

Illustration 11 shows Overton's right arm coming down, across his chest, and pulling down toward his left hip bone. He is still in balance as he reverses after the throw.

Overton follows through with his weight on his bent right leg. He is in control and has good balance (Illustration 12).

As shown in Illustration 13, momentum carries Overton on around as he finishes his reverse. Usually he takes one or two additional hops on his right foot to stop his momentum and leaves the ring out the back.

WEEKLY TRAINING PROGRAM AT LOS ALTOS

Warm-Up—Jogging and some striding. Push-ups, double sit-ups, stretching, and various limbering exercises. In our warm-ups, complete body looseness is emphasized. Usually the warm-up is done by the team prior to practice. Jump rope for five minutes each day. Weight training after practice. Check with the coach for sprint work after practice.

Monday—Twenty-five throws without reversing—emphasizing high lift over the front leg. Emphasis is placed on throwing against a stiff post leg (front) and going up and over it. We stress the action of the discus leaving the hand before the right (drive) leg leaves the ground. Work is done on locking the left side of the body and thrusting against it.

Work is also done on turning into the first step with emphasis on slow to fast acceleration. Throw 50 to 60 times with full action emphasizing good form and high flight.

Tuesday — Warm-Up—Thirty-five to 40 hard throws in a series of four. Speed is stressed in some of these series with flight, lift, and follow in others. We feel it is necessary for a young thrower to stress constantly one or two phases of his throw in each series. It is difficult to throw all-out on all throws and to develop the smoothness and coordination for top throwing. We certainly feel that throwing full-blast stressing every phase of the act of throwing the discus is necessary and our throwers throw that way in the last 15 or so throws. Our theory is, if a fault creeps into a thrower's form, the best way to iron it out is to go back and stress some of the basic fundamentals and then go back to the whole action and see if the trouble has been corrected. Sometimes it takes as many as 12 throws to pinpoint the flaw and to use the right kind of terminology to get the point across to the thrower.

Tuesday is usually the hardest throwing day and it is also used as a review day. Staying low, hip action, speed, getting into position, high flight, square shoulders, arm carry, release, post leg, and acceleration in a wide variety of drills are emphasized. We find that good form in the discus is difficult to maintain without resorting to the fundamentals constantly. Work is done on keeping the discus behind the hip during the spin and leading with the hips and body, especially on Mondays and Tuesdays.

Wednesday — Warm-Up—We stress speed work on this day and staying in the ring. Twenty-five to 35 throws are usually taken by our throwers emphasizing the whole action and staying in the ring. Thirty minutes of throwing are stressed without a reverse and work on staying low and lifting. If the thrower feels like throwing more, another hour of circle work is done.

We work closely with the discus throwers particularly on Mondays and Wednesdays. A coach must be with the discus men at least an hour a day to check them out in their form and to help correct the never-ending bad form habits they seem to fall into. Due to the light weight of the high school discus we work a great deal on the release and flight angle.

Mental preparation is emphasized for practice days and we try to have each workout anticipated with eagerness. A discus thrower must learn to really *put out* in each workout if optimum results are expected.

Thursday—Warm-Up—Throw lightly and work on position and smoothness for a few minutes. Sometimes our throwers do not throw at all on Thursday and rest completely for the meet on Friday. If there is no meet on Friday, we continue with Monday's workout.

Workouts are changed to adapt to different situations when necessary. Sometimes it is necessary to work on the other events to break the routine. Often our workout is changed completely and we go into a type of competition workout using handicaps in distance, etc. The coaches try to make the discus workouts fun.

7

COMMON ERRORS IN THE DISCUS

George Dunn
Oaklawn, Illinois, Community High School

A great deal has been written on the discus yet very little has been mentioned concerning the correction of faulty technique.

The common sense errors we have experienced most frequently are listed, and an attempt has been made to list the possible corrections. These are tips and information which have come from experience, clinics, talks with successful coaches and athletes, track magazines, and textbooks.

All corrections are for a right-handed athlete.

1. **Falling off balance while turning.** a) This begins at the back of the circle. The thrower's feet must never be wider than his shoulders. b) The weight must be over the left foot throughout the start of the turn at the back of the circle. c) A thrower should slow down at the back and start slowly.

2. **Landing off balance at the center of the circle.** a) Keep the eyes on a horizontal level or on the discus. b) Work off the left foot; keep the weight balanced and over the left foot at the back of the circle. c) Think of running or driving into the turn. d) Slow down until balance has improved.

3. **Permitting the discus to get in front or ahead as the thrower turns.** a) The legs take the body through the turn. Do not lead with the shoulder. b) A discus thrower should keep his knees close together as he starts into the turn with the right foot and toes pointing down for a *quick right foot.* c) Be sure the discus is in a good catch position before starting the turn. The right shoulder should be behind and stay behind the right hip throughout the turn. d) Feel the discus drag throughout the turn.

4. **Hopping rather than running or driving to the center of the circle.** a) Start low, and keep the butt in (squat down as a quarterback does under the center at the back of the circle). b) Keep the right foot down until the left foot points to the front of the circle at the beginning of the turn. c) Keep the knees close together when going into the turn with the right foot and toes pointing down for a *quick right foot.*

5. **Stopping or settling at the front of the circle.** a) Stay low, start low, and use a quick left foot. b) Drive up and over the left leg. Do not drop the left shoulder or collapse the left leg.

6. **Scooping the discus.** a) Be sure the discus is above the waist. b) Make certain the left shoulder is slightly higher than the right shoulder. c) Be sure that the preliminary swing is horizontal. d) Relax, do not try to muscle the swing. e) The thrower should be sure that his balance is correct and he is working over the left leg.

7. **Falling off balance at the front of the circle.** Be sure that the body weight is over the left leg at the back of the circle and balance is correct.

8. **Discus flutters or butterflies in flight.** a) Relax, do not grip the discus too hard. b) Keep the wrist straight.

9. **Discus turning over, with the right side lifting up and over.** a) Do not muscle or force the discus. b) Balance at the start of the spin and having the weight over the left leg prevents falling away or to the left. c) Do not pull away from the discus. Drive up and over the left leg. d) Keep the left shoulder above the right shoulder.

10. **Discus going to the right.** a) The discus is being released too soon, which is caused by poor foot position and balance. b) Be sure that the left leg is not blocking the hips. Work over the left leg at the back of the circle. c) Keep the left shoulder above the right shoulder.

11. **Left foot in the bucket.** Work over the left leg. A thrower's weight should be over his left leg at the back of the circle.

12. **No height on the discus while in flight.** The legs drive the discus up. A thrower should learn that his legs must be used to give height to the discus. Both legs must explode and drive the discus upward at the right moment.

13. **Tail of the discus is too low.** a) The discus is dropped below the hip level. b) Press the thumb down to keep the discus flat.

14. **Fouling at the front of the circle.** a) The left leg must be braced. b) Drop the body weight low immediately after the throw. c) A thrower should be sure that he is not crowding the front of the circle.

15. **Wind.** a) Head wind: Keep the discus height low, but not lower than 25°. Keep it flat. b) Tail Wind: Throw at maximum height of 42° to 45° and keep the discus flat. c) Right-handed wind: Keep the discus angle small (right side tilted up) and a normal angle in height flight. d) Left-handed wind: Attempt to get the left side of the discus higher, left side tilted up, and a normal angle in flight height.

Most errors originate with the initial move of the athlete at the back of the circle. If a discus thrower has a good foundation in technique, and masters those important little essentials at the start of the turn, he will develop few faults through his turns or spin. Another factor which needs constant emphasis is that he must relax.

8

ANALYSIS OF VAN REENEN'S DISCUS THROW

Willard Huyck
Carleton College

John Van Reenen, 1968 and 1969 NCAA discus champion from Washington State University, is shown throwing in the 1969 NCAA Meet at the University of Tennessee, Knoxville, Tennessee.

With his senior year coming up and already ranked seventh in the 1969 *Track and Field News* world ranking, John presents a brilliant, exciting potential. He has youth, 22 years of age, good size, 6 feet, 7 inches and 265 pounds, proven competitive excellence, a personal best of 107 feet, 6 inches and continually improving technique. As a freshman he threw 185 feet, 198 feet as a sophomore, and 207 feet as a junior last year.

After a promising junior shot putting career in South Africa, John has been coached by Jack Mooberry, the capable and respected coach at Washington State.

Coach Mooberry feels that John has excellent hands and imparts consistently good flight to the discus, has the rangy frame common to good discus throwers, and the concentration and desire to excel that will bring continued improvement. Jack thinks that although Van Reenen is strong now, he puts the shot 63 to 64 feet, he can develop increased strength. With a standing throw of 190 feet, increased efficiency in the turn can be exploited, and in using the entire circle, throwing through the discus, John can find significant improvement.

Before looking closely at the illustrations, it should be mentioned that any one sequence may or may not demonstrate the repeated good habits or weaknesses of the athlete. In analyzing the illustrations, as in coaching, one

Van Reenen's discus throw: Illustrations 1-4.

Van Reenen's discus throw (con't): Illustrations 5-8.

Van Reenen's discus throw (con't): Illustrations 9-12.

Van Reenen's discus throw (con't): Illustrations 13-16.

should be concerned with consistent techniques and beware of generalizing from one instance. Also, there may be no other event in which continuity is more critical and it is difficult to catch the fluid, continuous essence of good discus throwing from a set of very good pictures.

Illustrations 1-3. Van Reenen sets up an easy rhythm and gets the discus well behind him before initiating the turn. We cannot see it here, but hopefully he used an easy preliminary swing or two, not the series of tense, fast, contorted swings that one sees all too often. It is interesting that he stands erect before beginning his turn rather than staying relatively low (Illustrations 1 and 2).

Ilustrations 4-6. Van Reenen begins his turn with the discus well behind him, his feet taking the lead, and his weight moving over his left foot. Illustrations 4 and 5 give the impression that he does a hammer turn—that is, on the heel of his left foot, rather than on the toe or the ball of the foot—but Coach Mooberry says he does not do this often. As shown in Illustration 6, John's weight is well over his left leg as his right leg is pulled away from the ground.

Illustrations 7-9. The running turn or running rotation is beautifully displayed. Illustration 7 shows a true sprint position, bent right knee driven close to the left leg. As shown in Illustration 9, Van Reenen arrives in the center of the circle well closed with the discus behind him. His weight is nicely balanced over his right leg, but we wonder if he would not have been better off in a slightly lower position.

Illustrations 10-13. As shown in Illustration 10, John's right arm is still well back, perhaps 90° behind his hips, but, in seeing the difference between Illustrations 10 and 11, we wonder if he had the brilliant, fast hip action common to other great throwers of his period. However, Van Reenen has not rushed his arm action. Illustration 12 shows that John's head and chest are up and leading his forces up and out in the direction in which he wants the discus to go. The discus is released at shoulder height with the entire body lifted high and erect. (Illustration 13).

Illustrations 14-16. Van Reenen follows through, but it looks as though he may not have had the total explosion through the throw that one would like. Does he use the whole circle?

It is easy to sit back and dissect a fine athlete's technique; however, it is difficult and rare to find an able, fundamentally sound, well-motivated thrower, one of proven excellence in the distance he has thrown and in winning competition among national quality throwers. John Van Reenen is this type of thrower, and we can only look forward to even greater things from him this season and in the future.

9

DISCUS FORM OF AN OLYMPIC CHAMPION

M. E. Easton
University of Kansas

Illustration 1 shows Oerter in his initial stance facing the rear of the circle slightly to the right of the middle. Normally his back is more erect, but the muddy throwing surface required a low position for balance. His weight is evenly distributed on both feet in this low position.

As he executes his initial turn his weight shifts back, his left arm opens up, and the discus begins its backward movement into a cocked position. Oerter's right arm is relaxed at all times. He exerts no effort to keep the discus high, but holds it even with his right hip.

Notice that his center of gravity is well behind his heels, enabling him to progress, with his turn, toward the front of the ring.

As the turn progresses, his weight shifts back and onto the toes of his left foot. He is now leading his turn with his left knee and hip, and pulling with his left arm. Notice the 90° bend in his right leg which will remain constant regardless of the stage of his throw until he contracts it to some degree, as shown in Illustration 7, to avoid a jerky throw.

As shown in Illustration 3, Oerter is making his turn over his left foot with his right leg coming off the ground and initiating the turn as it heads for a plant position slightly forward and to the left of the middle of the ring. It should be noticed here that, under ordinary circumstances, Illustration 3 would be eliminated from these sequence shots as Oerter would be executing his turns much more quickly and the sequence would be from Illustration 2 to Illustration 4. Due to the muddy ring conditions, Oerter had to slow down to avoid slipping and to attain a good throwing position. The criticism in this case would be that he is spending too much time on the ground, thus taking away his quick turn. His left arm is still pulling and the discus is well back at hip level. The low position of the discus keeps his arm relaxed and facilitates balance, enabling him to turn quickly in a smooth, uninterrupted motion.

In Illustration 4, as Oerter's right foot heads for the plant position, his body has an extreme forward lean and his left arm is now coming back next to his body. This position forms a more compact unit of the body, enabling the thrower to turn with balance and land in a set position, poised for a more powerful delivery. Notice the height of his right knee and foot—no conscious effort is made to raise the right leg high and jump, but concentration is on a quick, well-balanced turn, while staying off the ground for as short a time as possible. Oerter strives for a low position throughout the turn and, as a result, is able to get maximum spring from his legs at the moment of delivery.

Illustration 5 shows Oerter landing on a bent right leg. His left arm and shoulder are held in and bent at a 90° angle. The discus is still well back but is now in a higher position. As the thrower begins to set for his throw, his right arm shows the first signs of strain. A concentrated effort is made to stay in a compact unit until the moment of delivery.

As shown in Illustration 6, Oerter's left hip and arm initiate the opening up for the delivery. The discus is now in its highest position but is still well back, and his arm is straight and about to start its downward arc for the hip delivery (Illustration 8). Notice the position of the thrower's head—up, but not leading the throw. An effort is made to keep it back, in the same manner that the discus is delayed, until final delivery. Notice the slight extension of Oerter's right leg from its original 90° angle which enables him to come into a more upright position, and check his forward momentum so a foul will not result.

In Illustration 7, Oerter's left arm is extended to enable him to come into an almost upright position at the front of the circle. His right leg now settles or contracts to facilitate a smooth delivery by driving off this bent leg with power. Notice the change in Oerter's head position and eye level. The discus is still well back, but is now in its downward path toward his right hip from where it is delivered.

Illustration 8 shows Oerter delivering from hip level, still pulling with his left arm and leading with his left hip. His head and eyes are up at the desired level or flight of the discus as his entire left side precedes the discus. His left foot is planted slightly to the left of center but close enough to the front of the ring to enable him to use as much of the ring as possible and still not foul on his reverse movement. His left leg is planted slightly to the left of the center line, as mentioned previously, with an approximate left toe, right heel center line relationship. His left arm is now bent but is still pulling the discus

Discus Form of an Olympic Champion

Discus Form of an Olympic Champion

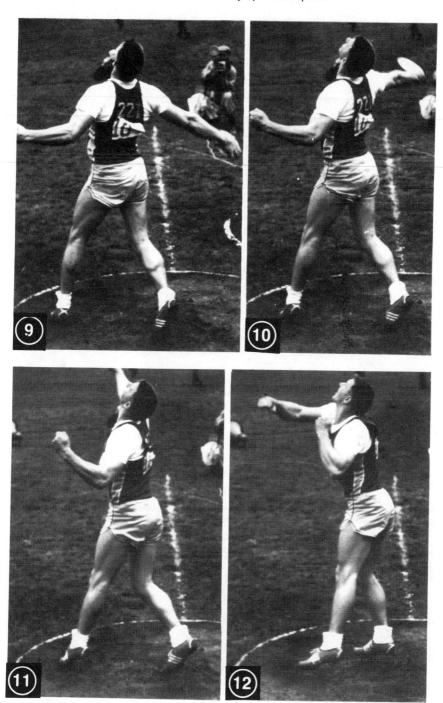

on through. Oerter's bent left arm generates a more rapid whip of his right arm and the discus. His right hip is driven up and forward and the upper body continues to rotate with the pull of his left arm as the throw progresses. Notice the thrower's head and eye level.

As shown in Illustration 10, Oerter is driving off his right leg, starting his reverse, and forcing his body up and over his now almost straight left leg. His left arm has stopped pulling and remains in a bent position for balance, enabling him to keep his shoulders square which in turn eliminates a pull away from the discus.

Illustration 11 shows a continuation or follow-through of the throw, demonstrating the power turned on at the climax of Oerter's throw. Notice his now relaxed right leg and strained left leg as the throw nears its completion. His head and eye level are still up as he follows the flight of the discus.

In Illustration 12, Oerter is shown with both feet off the ground about to complete his reverse movement. His eyes are still on the flight of the discus as his body returns once again to a compact, well-balanced unit by bringing his right arm in close to his body.

Illustration 13 shows Oerter balancing on his right leg as his reverse is completed after the throw. Notice that Oerter's concentration is still on the flight of the discus. His arms are relaxed and away from his body to offer him balance and to prevent a foul throw.

10
USING THE WIND IN DISCUS THROWING

Jim Napier
United States Air Force

Learning how to use different wind directions as effectively as possible is an important part of discus throwing technique. The discus is shaped so the wind is able to hold it up in the air, causing the discus to sail farther, providing it is thrown in an advantageous direction in relation to the direction of the wind. The accompanying diagrams should help illustrate which throwing directions, in relation to wind direction and velocity, are an advantage and how to use effectively the different directions, which affect the flight of the discus.

A discus thrower can have a better understanding of different wind directions, and how they effect the flight of the discus by using them in practice whenever possible. He should be alert in observing the way different wind directions affect the discus in both flight and distance.

The discus thrower should keep a record of the distances he achieves when using the various wind directions. Thus, he will have some idea as to which throwing directions in relation to wind directions will be the most

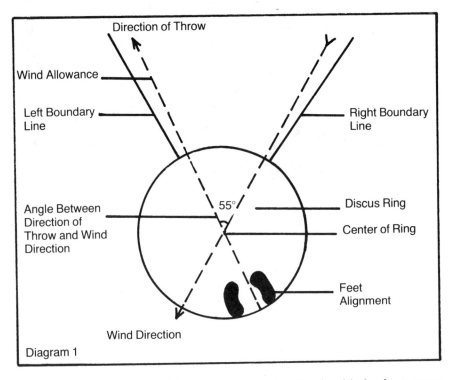

Diagram 1

advantageous for him and his style of throwing. He should also have some idea how to cope with a wind disadvantage in order to achieve the most efficient throw possible.

When using the wind, body alignment in relation to the direction of the throw is important for an accurate and effective throw. As shown in Diagram 1, an imaginary line, running between the feet, through the center of the ring and out toward the throwing area will establish the direction of the throw. To find out where the feet should be placed for the throw will require a little study of the sector, wind velocity, and a survey of the area, similar to that used by a golfer in lining up a long putt. The technique used in body alignment for a selected throwing direction is basically the same as lining up for any throw, regardless of wind direction or velocity. Only slight modifications should be made, especially in excessive winds or wind directions that affect the flight of the discus adversely.

After the discus thrower determines which direction he will be throwing into in relation to the different wind directions, he should learn to be confident of the throwing direction in relation to the way he is lined up in the ring. This will help eliminate as many inefficient throws as possible while increasing consistency in both distance and range of the throws.

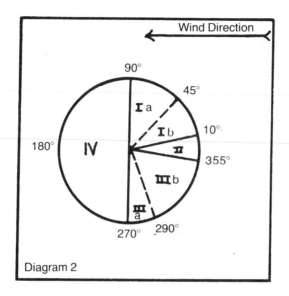

Diagram 2

Diagram 2 shows which throwing directions are more effective in relation to the different wind directions, and how they affect the flight of the discus. The center of the 360° circle represents the discus ring, and the area of the circle is the throwing area. The throwing area is marked off in six sectors. Each sector shows the different wind directions, and it will be noted the effect of the wind upon the discus in flight will be different for each sector. This diagram shows the importance of knowing which wind directions are an advantage and which are a disadvantage so the discus thrower will better understand how to use them. All the sectors discussed will relate to a right-handed discus thrower. To relate them to the left-handed discus thrower, the situations should be reversed.

In sectors la and lb (Diagram 2), there is a right- to left-hand wind in the 10° to 90° range. Throwing in this sector, or direction, will cause the discus to sail for a longer period of time than it would if thrown in any other sector, or direction, in relation to a different wind direction. There is more force underneath the discus than on top, and as it reaches the top of the arch, in its flight the discus will begin to turn on its side. The main idea in controlling the flight of the discus is to keep it level with the ground as long as possible, which will help insure a longer throw. When the forces that were applied to the discus begin to die out, it will turn on its side, until it is perpendicular with the ground. When this occurs, there will be no more lift on the discus, and there will be no force to stall it out, especially in the 45° to 90° range (sector la). The discus will continue it its original arch, adverse wind will be slight, and only gravity will be present to bring it down.

69

Using the Wind in Discus Throwing

The only disadvantage of a right- to left-hand wind direction, as far as actual competition is concerned, is the possibility of throwing the discus out of bounds. Sometimes the most favorable direction into which to throw is straight down the left boundary line of the sector. If the wind is from right to left, as it would be in sectors Ia and Ib, Diagram 2, the wind might carry the discus out of bounds if it is thrown parallel to the left boundary line of the sector. When selecting a direction into which to throw, the discus thrower should allow for the wind if the direction is close, or parallel to, one of the boundary lines of the sector.

As shown in sector II, Diagram 2, the wind is coming straight into the throwing area. This is called a head wind, and is probably the most difficult wind of which to take advantage. If the throw is too high, the back edge of the discus will drop and it will stall out before it reaches the top of the arch of its flight. This will cause the discus to fall too steeply from the arch, and a loss in distance might occur. To throw into a head wind, the discus should be released a few degrees lower in height than it should be in sectors Ia and Ib.

The angle of release of the discus is determined by how much the thrower's wrist is cocked as the discus is released. The direction of the wind and wind velocity in relation to the direction of the throw will determine how much the wrist should be cocked in order to keep the discus from stalling out too soon.

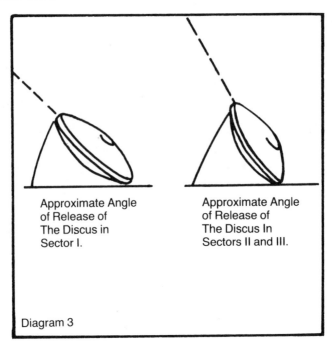

Approximate Angle of Release of The Discus in Sector I.

Approximate Angle of Release of The Discus In Sectors II and III.

Diagram 3

70

Diagram 3 shows the difference in angles of release between sectors I and sectors II, IIIa and IIIb; however, individual preference will determine the actual angles of release. The discus should be released at different angles of release, depending on wind velocity and direction of wind. By cocking the wrist more, when throwing in sector II, the discus can be kept level with the ground for a longer period of time which will help to prevent the wind from stalling the discus out too soon.

In sectors IIIa and IIIb, Diagram 2, the wind is a left to right-hand wind and is considered by most discus throwers to be a disadvantage. If the discus is released at the right height and angle in relation to the wind velocity, this wind can be used as an advantage, but only slightly, depending on the angle of release between the direction of the throw and the wind direction. The throw should be made in the 270° to 290° range, sector IIIa, if possible, for the best results. The effect of the wind will be less a factor at this angle and less stalling will occur. There is very little lift on the discus in sectors IIIa and IIIb except in the early stages of flight.

When throwing into the wind, as discussed in sectors Ia, Ib, II, IIIa and IIIb, there are two important points to remember: 1) the greater the angle between the direction of the throw and wind direction, the less stalling effect the wind will have on the discus; and 2) the greater the wind velocity, the greater the angle should be between the direction of the throw and the wind direction, but not more than 90°.

In sector IV, Diagram 2, the wind is called a tail wind, and is not considered an advantage. There is more force on top of the discus which tends to push it down. The best thing to do when throwing with the wind is to throw higher than normally and concentrate on right technique. The angle of release of the discus is not critical when throwing with the wind, since most of the force will be behind the discus, or on top, and there will be no stalling effect as there would be in sectors II, IIIa, IIIb, and part of I. This is the only advantage of a tail wind.

By studying each practice throw, the way the wind affects it, the distance obtained with each different wind direction and velocity, and the height and angle the discus is released in relation to the wind direction and velocity, a discus thrower should be able to improve his distance with the discus when the right conditions prevail.

Many coaches and spectators feel that the javelin throw is the most beautiful of all track and field events.

11
MECHANICS OF THE JAVELIN

Jerry Frasier
North Fulton High School, Atlanta, Georgia

Many coaches and spectators have said that the javelin is the most beautiful of all track and field events, and we are inclined to believe this statement. Watching a silver javelin travel through the air, appearing at times almost motionless, and then seeing it plunge to the ground past one of the white lines denoting 190, 200, etc., must be classified as one of the most exciting moments in track and field.

When we came to North Fulton in 1960, the school record for the javelin was 165 feet, set in the middle 40's. This record was a personal challenge to be conquered and fortunately last year we had a junior, Gary Gavant, who threw 190 feet to break this oldest school record.

We would like to divide this article into three sections:

- Selection of the thrower.
- Conditioning.
- Technique.

SELECTING THE THROWER

In selecting a boy who has a potential for throwing the javelin, the following three basic qualities are necessary in order to become a top-notch thrower.

• He must have a strong throwing arm. A good test, which shows a close correlation to determine a boy's throwing ability, is the softball throw. We have a physical fitness test in all of our eighth grade physical education classes, and one of the activities is the softball throw. If a boy is in the top five in eighth grade in the softball throw, and has the remaining qualities, he should be considered as a javelin prospect.

• He must have good speed (100-dash time) or at least a good start (20-yard) sprint time). Speed is an essential quality fo the javelin thrower.

• He must possess coordination and agility. These qualities are important in maneuvering the javelin into throwing position at the same time the feet

How important is size? We do not believe size is as important as the three previously mentioned qualities, but if a big man possesses these qualities, usually a good big man is better than a good little man.

CONDITIONING

• Running. If the boy does not participate in another sport, we advise the javelin throwers to train with the cross-country team during the fall and winter. Distance running is good for the development of general body conditioning. We also have our javelin throwers run a steep 30 yard hill 15 to 25 repeats a day. This hill helps to develop the power required of the legs.

Distance running, to a small degree, is continued until warm weather arrives in March. Then running is limited to sprints of 150, 80, and 60 yards and sprints up the hill.

• Weight Training. We have our javelin throwers work on weights three days a week, using exercises to strengthen their arms, chest, shoulders and backs. Basically, we use six exercises:

1. One-hand and two-arm pullovers, lying on the back on a bench with 50 to 75 pounds of weight.
2. Bench presses (poundage as much as a boy can handle).
3. Rows (100 to 150 pounds).
4. Dead lifts (100 to 200 pounds).
5. Presses (boys use as much weight as possible).
6. One of our weight exercises may be unique in that one of the barbells are fitted on is taken to the field where the boys throw it, about 10 yards, as they do the javelin. This exercise gives weight resistance to the muscle groups that are directly involved in actual throwing.

TECHNIQUE IN THE LAST STRIDE OF THE RUN-UP

At North Fulton, the Finnish five-step front cross-over is used. We are convinced that this is the best style of throwing for two reasons: more drive off the throwing leg; more quick body rotation, which provides additional power for the upper body and the throwing arm.

To help the boys learn this cross-over, cut-out foot-print diagrams of the five basic steps are placed in position on the throwing field, and then they step through the maneuver until they are familiar with the procedure. One tip is to assume that the feet positions are the hands of the clock pointing in the direction of the hour.

In using the cross-over, the thrower should know exactly where to begin his maneuver (step A) in relation to the scratch line. If he starts too close to the scratch line, he may be over the line before completion of the cross-over and vice versa (Diagram 1).

Our throwers are instructed to work out their cross-over about six feet from the scratch line from (step F) reverse. The reason is apparent if the throwers fall forward and go over the scratch line.

After a javelin thrower has worked at his cross-over, he should measure from the scratch line to step A and place a peg or check mark on the side of the approach chute with the foot that assumes step A. If he is right handed, step A will be taken with his left foot so the check mark will be on the left side of the approach chute. This mark should be constant and measured before each completion.

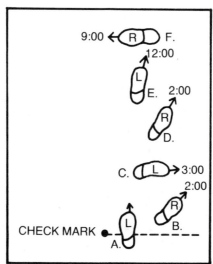

Diagram 1.

We also have a check mark at the beginning of the approach run. This distance is measured from the step A check mark. The approach run will vary with different individuals, but it should be long enough to insure a completely relaxed and controlled all-out run when the thrower reaches the step A check mark.

After the boy understands the cross-over, he is given a javelin. He is asked to grab the top part of the binding closest to the tail, in a comfortable position, with the shaft of the javelin in the middle of his hand, near his wrist. Now the javelin is parallel with his forearm. Usually, the boy will use one of three basic grips:

- Index finger overlapping the top of the binding with the other fingers wrapped around the binding.
- Middle finger lapping over the end of the binding, with the index finger along the top of the shaft for balance.
- The binding nestled between the index finger and the middle finger.

In the approach run, our throwers are instructed to hold the javelin above their heads, with the elbow forming about a 90 degree angle. The point of the javelin should be tilted slightly upward and held in position in the direction of the run. The thrower's eyes can check the point of the javelin to see that it does not turn during the approach run. If it does turn, the alignment of the javelin will be off when it is thrown.

When the thrower is taking the C step, the javelin should be dropped back to a position parallel with his arm, which should be extended almost straight. The thrower's body should be rotated to the right side of the chute on step D, and the javelin quickly pulled over the top of his body close to his right ear. His head should lean to the left to enable the javelin to be brought to as near the center of his body's center of gravity as possible. The longer and greater the pull of the arm, the more power will be put on the javelin. It should be released at about a 40 to 42 degree angle, off the right foot (step D) and a simultaneous shift to the left foot (step E). After the javelin has been released, a quick reverse or step F insures a powerful follow-through.

In order to receive the benefit of all mechanics, the javelin should be thrown directly in front of the thrower. When the javelin lands, the point should be pointing directly at the thrower. If the tail of the javelin points to the right or left of the thrower during the throw, he may check the tip for proper release.

A prospective javelin thrower should use the distance rated javelin for two reasons: first, there is less vibration in flight; second, there is a shallower angle on the landing

In trying to cover an event as complicated as the javelin in limited space, much is not said that should be, but we hope some tips that will be helpful have been given.

12

THE EUROPEAN TECHNIQUE

Ed Tucker
U.S. Coast Guard Academy

Regarding form for throwing a javelin, there are two basically different types of throwers, the arm thrower and the body thrower. The arm thrower is generally the American who has a super strong arm that was developed by throwing a football or a baseball. With only a few days of basic training, he can throw the javelin and throw it well in dual meet competition. The distance is almost directly related to his arm strength, with form, as the Europeans see it, entering very little into the picture. This type of throwing almost dominates the javelin throwers of our nation's high schools and the majority of college throwers.

The body thrower uses, as the term says, all of his body in a well-timed coordinated effort. This system is obviously due to the addition of the pwerful leg muscles, and hip. plus the lower and upper torso all acting before the arm. The arm, in this case, when it enters into the throw, is the *icing on the cake.*

In discussing form, a little background as to how and when this new system was developed may be of help. Kalevi Rompotti, a famous Finnish coach, presented this system to the newly formed World Track and Field Clinic in 1956. His main change was to alter the position of the hip shoulder relationship to the scratch line. Prior to this time, a thrower's hips and shoulders (both parallel to each other) were perpendicular to the scratch line, but he said this was not conducive to using the entire body. In his presentation, he said the hip should be parallel to the scratch line and the shoulders perpendicular to both the hips and the foul line. In reality, the hips are at an angle of about 30 degrees to the scratch line even though the thrower is attempting to keep them parallel (Diagram 1). Prior to using the new system, the Finns also used a cross-over step which caused their hips to be near perpendicular to the scratch line.

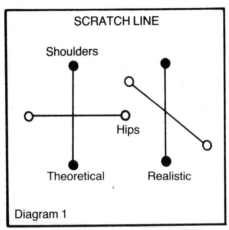

Diagram 1

Finnish coaches had a great deal of trouble during the first three or four years when they tried to initiate this type of throwing. These difficulties were encountered because it takes many months of constant throwing (using the new technique) before throwers become efficient. It is not a natural position, so it must be learned. In the early years, Finland did not have training nets so the athletes had to attempt to learn this new form during the late spring and while competing in the summer. It simply did not work, and in the late 50's and early 60's the Finnish javelin throwers did very poorly in national competition. Around 1962, Finland went to the training net concept and the throwing of overweighted objects. But more important that the power development gained by all the throwing was the ability to work on the new technique over a period of seven to eight months prior to competition. In this way, the dynasty of Finnish javelin throwers, which has reigned for the last 12 years, was started.

Once the new system was mastered, the average distance of the good thrower picked up 40 to 50 feet. In the case of a few exceptions, their performance increased over 80 feet. The Finns initiated this technique over 15 years ago and it has now spread over Europe. For this reason we will, from this point on in the article, refer to the body thrower as using the European technique.

As the accompanying illustrations are analyzed, we will try to bring out the theoretical, and then the good and weak points of the thrower in each sequence.

In the run or final approach (Illustration 1), a thrower must concentrate on keeping his feet pointing straight ahead. At the time the right foot lands on completing the first of the final four steps, the javelin is back and in the throwing position, the arm is extended but relaxed with the palm up and in the orthodox Finnish grip, and the shoulders are turned parallel to the javelin. The javelin is well controlled with the tip at eye level and close to the head. The thrower's left foot lands and the speed rhythm must accelerate during the last two steps.

At this stage the thrower is in excellent position. His feet are pointing straight ahead, and the javelin is in the proper position in full readiness for the throw.

A thrower should push with his left leg into the third throwing step with a high, strong, forward lift of the right knee. This slight pause in rhythm allows a little extra time for the final left foot almost to catch up with the right foot which will soon land. An attempt is made to have the left foot strike the ground as soon as possible after the right. The thrower's hips should be almost parallel to the scratch line, with his shoulders twisted almost 80 degrees to the hips (Illustration 2).

The thrower's hips and shoulders are in excellent position. His arm is back and the javelin is still in great alignment for a super throw. His right knee, however, does not lift high enough. Thus, he does not have the time he needs to get into the proper landing position.

As shown in Illustration 3, the competitor is in mid-air and is awaiting his landing on the right foot. There is a slight pause before the split-second sequence of events which will follow. As mentioned previously, the arm must be relaxed and flexible. If the whip is to take place, the thrower's arm cannot in any way pull prematurely, be excessively tight, or in any way cut down on the whip effect.

The thrower is in good position except for his lack of backward lean which is so important. His feet are still pointing forward and his javelin is in the proper position.

Upon touching the ground with his right foot, the thrower's body should be leaning backward at an angle of approximately 30 degrees, which enables him to better use the power of his leg and trunk muscles. The motion of the left foot toward the ground is accomplished by extending the leg forward (reaching out) and landing on the heel in order to stop as quickly as possible. The faster a thrower runs and the quicker he can stop, the greater upper body whip he will develop.

The thrower in Illustration 4 is reaching perfectly with his left leg for the ground and his foot direction is also very good. However, it can be seen clearly that he is now paying for his error made earlier by not leaning back enough. When his left foot reaches the ground, he will be almost vertical to the ground. His left arm has also drifted up and out prior to the touching of the left foot.

As the thrower's left leg reaches the ground with the ankle straight forward, the jolt takes place (Illustration 5). The leg must stop the momentum instantly and this is where the great throws begin. If a thrower has a fast run but cannot stop the lower part of his body quickly, it means that he will run over his left leg and receive almost no whip upon release. In a split second the following things happen: The right leg punches the hip forward quickly and down slightly to place the body in the bow or horseshoe position, the torso comes forward violently in response to the whip, and the throw is now ready for the waiting arm. As the rush of the body on the left foot is completed, only then does the hand begin its pull. It will be noticed that in the good throws, the thrower's chest has reached far forward, while the throwing hand remains behind the back.

Again the thrower shows excellent foot position. His right heel has turned outward, which shows good hip action, and his left foot is planted firmly in the direction of the throw. His arm has stayed back in great fashion waiting for the balance of his body to complete its part of the throw. It appears that the release will not be as high (distance from the left foot to the right hand) as desired.

If the whip is extreme, which it should be if the hips drop and turn correctly and the left leg acted properly, the thrower's arm is automatically forced to come through quickly with a very high, whip-like release directly over his head (Illustration 6). This is really what it is all about. The faster the arm (velocity) and the higher the release, the greater the distance achieved. This can be explained by physics in that the velocity is increased as to the cube of the radius. In this case the radius is the distance between the left foot and the right hand on release. Thus, it can be seen that a release four to five inches higher than normal means a fantastic increase in velocity and obviously greater distance.

The thrower tends to be bent over and not up over his left foot at the time of release. This hurt him in regard to getting the longest possible radius and therefore cut down on his velocity. His left leg is still not vertical with the ground, yet the javelin has already left his hand.

Upon release, the thrower's body should be fully extended off his left leg with the body being as tall as possible (Illustration 7). As mentioned previously, this high release is a key point. When the body momentum passes beyond the planted left foot, the thrower's right foot comes forward in its role to stop the body from passing over the scratch line. The angle of release was established by his ability to keep the tip of the javelin alongside his eyes during the final part of the throw.

In illustration 6 the angle appeared perfect, but in this illustration it seems that he might have pulled down on release which causes the tail of the javelin to drop and changes the angle of flight.

As shown in Illustration 8, the thrower's upper body in its follow-through motion drops forward, down, and to the left. His right leg must get into position quickly to stop the forward motion of the body.

At this time the thrower is in good position to stop himself. His body momentum is also going in the exact direction of the javelin, which shows he did not allow it to slip off to the side.

The final phase of the throw (Illustration 9) is simply bringing the body to a complete halt before reaching the foul line. This is done by pushing back with the planted right foot.

The thrower finished in ideal position. He is close to the foul line but was not cramped in his final steps. All in all, it was a very good throw and the technique he used very well sums up the European style of throwing. His foot position was always good, his arm and javelin carry excellent, his backward lean could have been a little more, and upon release he could have been a little taller which would have given him a higher release.

In summary, we think it can be seen that this technique is one that requires a great deal of practice to perfect because it is not a natural position. This is why it is necessary for a javelin thrower to throw and throw correctly for many months prior to competition in order to learn and fortify the proper form if he wishes to achieve great success in the javelin.

13
JAVELIN THROWING—
SAM COLSON STYLE

Fred Wilt
Editor of Track Technique

When the University of Kansas superb left-handed javelin thrower, Sam Colson, threw 290 feet, 10 inches in 1973, he clearly identified himself as a world-class performer in this event. Most throwers use 14 to 17 approach strides before delivery. Only the final five strides of the run up are shown in this sequence.

Coleson has already withdrawn the spear from an over-the shoulder carry position prior to the action shown in Illustration 1. Illustrations 1 through 8 show that Colson used two so-called cross-steps in arriving in his throwing stride. Notice that he has correctly lost effective contact with his rear (left) foot before the right foot has been planted (Illustration 8). He has run away from his left arm (Illustration 9), evoking a powerful eccentric contraction (forced stretching) of the muscles in this throwing limb. Notice the left arm appears bent (Illustration 6). This is a common fault. However, the leaving behind of this limb before arriving in the taut bow position formed by his left leg, hips, torso, and left arm (Illustration 9), leads one to believe this arm has correctly stretched to an athletically straight position roughly parallel to the ground.

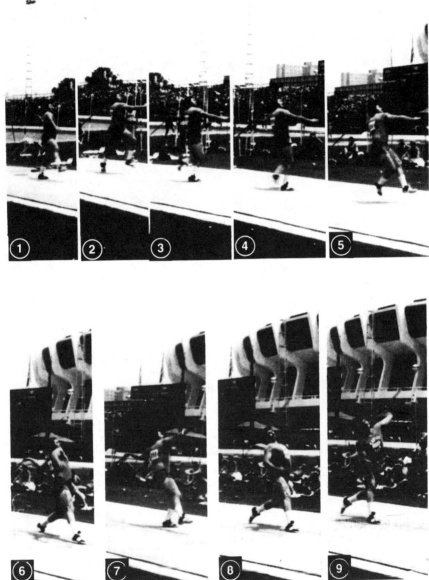

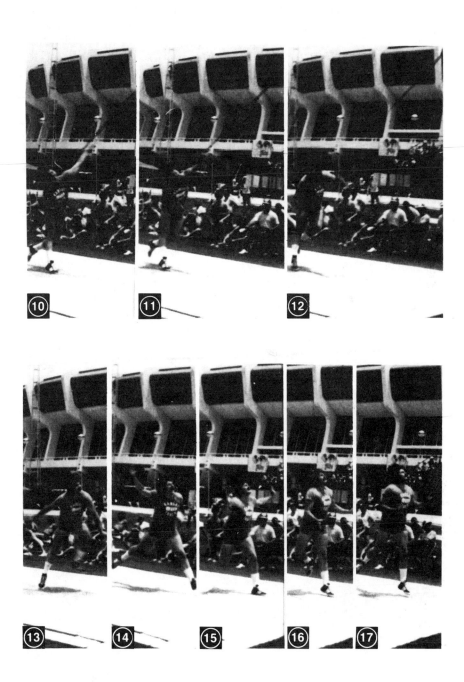

In the throwing action proper (Illustration 9 and 10), the left arm correctly strikes late and fast, after all weight is off the rear foot, the chest has turned to the front in the direction of the throw, the horizontal axes passing from side to side through the hips and the shoulders are roughly parallel, and the body weight is over the front leg. The elbow of the throwing (left) arm rises higher than the wrist during the early part of the action of this arm, between what is shown in Illustrations 9 and 10, as the missile is released above the left shoulder between Illustrations 10 and 11. It is interesting to notice that Colson's right leg is almost unbent as it is being planted (Illustration 8), it bends slightly (Illustration 9), and finally extends (straightens) powerfully (Illustration 10), just as the missile is directly above the body's center of gravity in a technically correct delivery action. What is shown in Illustration 1-17 is simply Colson's successful effort to remain behind the scratch-line to avoid fouling, and has no part of the throwing action. However, it does indicate a desirable continuity of momentum.

It is sometimes suggested that javelin throwing may be described as the European style, American method, Finnish style or whatever. Such classifications are as antiquated as knee-length bloomers for female athletes. The basic principles and especially advanced mechanical, physiological, and aerodynamic details of javelin throwing as understood today are now well-documented via the printed page and slow-motion movie film, and readily available to everyone. Thus javelin technique is now universally known. However, there will always be variations of correct technique according to individual differences of athletes. Regardless, we seldom see athletes with the performance potential of Sam Colson.

14
THE JAVELIN—
FINNISH STYLE

Ed Tucker
U.S. Coast Guard Academy

The United States had a fantastic showing in track and field in Mexico City but how about the javelin? Why are the javelin throwers so poor when we have 200 million people in our country and the major school athletic activities involve throwing activities? We consider football and baseball as basic games whereas Europeans are mainly involved with soccer or foot type activities, yet they out-throw us. Why?

It is a combination of a completely different philosophy about training and a more efficient throwing technique.

Weight-lifting has had a great influence on the success of the field events in this country. Events such as the shot put and discus have been directly improved through the tremendous strength and size of the modern athlete. But, in that the javelin is listed as a weight event, the weight-training program generally comprises the major portion of the off-season training. The concept in this country on javelin training is the same as it has been for the last 10 or 15 years, and that is a thrower works to develop strength in the throwing muscles. He will use pulleys or weights that will work on the various muscle groups and specialize primarily on the strength of the triceps, shoulder, and general throwing muscles.

It is not strength but power that counts. To clarify the two terms, strength means the maximum force applied in a single muscular contraction, but power is the ability to release maximum muscular force in the shortest period of time. The same parallel can be drawn to a fast ball pitcher in baseball. When the resistance is low (baseball or javelin), it is the speed of delivery which counts, not the strength of the throwing arm. The big difference then between concepts is we tend to feel that strength will cause an increase in speed but the Finns developed a program which works specifically on the power of their throwers.

Before discussing the Finnish program, we would like to list some common American quotations: "It is better to throw hard two days than throw five days easy." "The javelin is a pull, not a throw." "Build up the momentum but do not lose it. Use it."

As Bud Held said: "In the American system it is difficult to maintain speed after step one because of the complicated movements required in getting into position. Many throwers gradually slow down during the last three or four steps. The thrower must make every effort to maintain his speed and still get into position."

What is the basic difference between the American style and the Finnish style? The main difference is the hip position. For clarification as to steps, as the right foot lands on the first of the final four steps it is called 1, left 2, final right 3, and the braking final 4. The American style is characterized by a relatively short and low third cross step with the trunk turned to the right and deeply bent at the hips. In the third step the biggest essential difference between the Finnish and the American (Held) style will be noticed. In Held's style, in the second throwing step, the left leg steps on the ground with the toes clearly pointed more inward, so that the foot makes a greater angle with the throwing line, due to turning the hips to the right. It is harder then to push strongly with the left leg to the third throwing step, as is done in the Finnish style. The push of the left leg to the third throwing step is rendered in the Finnish style with a high and strong forward push of the right knee, with the effect that the right hip stays continuously in a line about at right angles to the direction of throw. However, the upper body is turned to the right so much that the shoulder line is parallel with the throwing line. In order to get the right rhythm and get the right knee better forward, the right knee already in the first throwing step is often pushed more up and forward. The upper body turn to the right is helped with the left arm pushing it backward. When the right leg is coming to the ground for the third throwing step, in the Finnish style, the hip and shoulder lines are perpendicular to each other, while in the Held style they are in the same line (Diagram 1).

The faster a javelin thrower runs and the quicker he can stop, the greater upper body whip he will develop. The major reason why the Finns like their style is that it is easier to maintain a fast rate of speed while going through the last four steps, in that the feet are pointing forward and there are no cross-over problems. It is easy to maintain the speed of the thrower and the

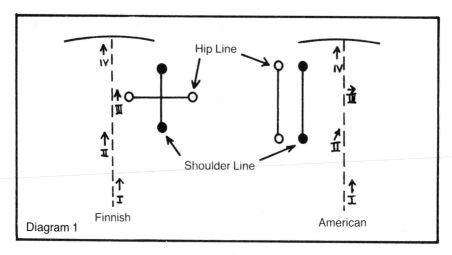

Hip Line

Shoulder Line

Diagram 1 Finnish American

hip is in the proper position. The old concept of having the hip turn 90°, thereby allowing more time to apply force to the javelin, is now obsolete. Because the javelin stays in the thrower's hand only a fraction of a second, the hip does not have time to rotate and then drive forward. In the Finnish system, the hip is already in position—they just have a quick extension of the leg. They stay low on the right leg driving the right hip up and forward. The hip is already parallel to the throwing line so they can concentrate on the movements of the chest and upper trunk (shoulder) which the Finns feel is more important than the movements of the hip in the last phase.

Their major problem in the javelin throw is how to land on the right foot at speed with the body well back and from there carry out a vicious, well-timed arm movement which is supported by a powerful body contribution. To accomplish this, the thrower lands on the heel of his right foot, the backward lean of his body is approximately 30°, and the right foot is pointing forward. The left arm is bent across the chest, the left elbow is high, and the thrower is looking forward and upward over the left shoulder. The right arm is extended, the hand held high, and the javelin's point kept down, parallel with the line of the shoulder. In a split second the following things happen: The right leg drives the hip violently forward and a conscious effort is on staying low on the leg, driving the hip forward and up. The left arm starts the upper body in motion as the left arm pulls violently to the left. Then the whole upper body and arm begin their part of the throw. The follow-through carries the head and upper body forward and down.

The footwork is (starting four steps out) longer but slower (1), shorter but faster (2), and the last two steps much faster but the thought is medium but fast (3), and then shorter, very fast (4) and throw. A javelin thrower must develop a rhythm and this will vary slightly with individuals. The main

The faster a javelin thrower runs and the quicker he can stop, the greater upper body whip he will develop.

thought is keeping the feet pointing straight ahead and using the hop-like approach after the second step to get the body in position.

In the typical Finnish throw, at the time the right foot lands on completing the first of the final steps, the javelin is back and in the throwing position. The arm is extended but relaxed and the shoulders are already turned parallel to the javelin. The javelin is well controlled, near the body, and in throwing position. The right leg makes a powerful push-off in preparation for the final steps. The left foot lands and drives forward and the fast speed continues. Speed rhythm must accelerate during the last two steps In the final two steps, the right leg is striving down to the ground, the pelvis is lowered. This enables the thrower to have a strong backward lean, thereby using the power in his leg and back. The throw must begin from below and as far behind as possible. The motion of the left foot toward the ground is done by extending the leg forward landing on the heel, in order to stop as quickly as possible. As the left leg reaches the ground with the ankle straight forward, the throw begins with the leg-hip, shoulder, and chest turning flash-like in the direction of the throw. The pull (throw), which began by exerting the right foot, is now continuing with the trunk, and the hand still remains inactive behind the back. As the rush of the body on the left foot is completed, only then does the hand begin its pull. It will always be noticed that the good throws find the chest has reached far forward while the throwing hand still remains behind the back.

Think what would happen if some of our 240-foot throwers started to use this sytem of training and throwing. Within several years, with all our natural talent, we are convinced the United States can control the event. We will never know unless people are willing to accept the fact that what we are doing definitely is not the system and give this highly proven system a try.

As a parallel thought, think back on how long it took for the fiber glass pole to be accepted. Perhaps the ball type training and the fiber glass pole will be two of a kind.

15
JAVELIN TRAINING PROGRAMS

John R. Fromm
Chief Sealth High School, Seattle, Washington

This article on training methods for javelin throwers has been excerpted from a master's thesis and is based upon the results of a questionnaire submitted to javelin throwers and coaches. Seventeen of the 20 throwers who had thrown over 250 feet in the period from 1956 through 1966 participated in the study. The track coaches questioned were those who had a thrower who achieved either a first, second or third in an NCAA meet or else at least two throwers who secured a fourth, fifth or sixth place in NCAA competition for the same period of years.

PRE-SEASON SUMMARY

Pre-Season Participation. The total number surveyed participated or, in the case of the coaches, advised a pre-season conditioning program in which the thrower prepares himself for javelin competition by an emphasis on general body conditioning. With such agreement the implication is fairly obvious; that is, if a thrower anticipates good throwing ability he must work for it, and he cannot wait until the competitive season begins to start conditioning his body and expect it to be in a condition of readiness for effective results.

Weight Training. Thirty-four respondents participated in a pre-season weight—lifting program. The individual programs varied but most emphasized body strength. Bench presses, sit-ups, bent arm pullovers, half-squats, and military presses were the exercises most utilized by the combined coaches and throwers, and are listed in the order of their popularity. It can be concluded that a weight training schedule varies for each individual and is determined primarily by indications of strengths and weaknesses. It can also be concluded that some exercises will provide a more general body conditioning than others, so this too is a determining factor when setting up a weight training program.

Isometric Program. As only 7 of the 39 coaches and throwers indicated participation in an isometric program as such, it was concluded that at the present time the isometric exercise program has not been fully utilized in the body conditioning program of the javelin thrower. However, it was not concluded that an isometric program has no value.

Running and Hurdling. Thirty-six participants included running or hurdling in the pre-season training program. Nineteen of the 36 recommended the inclusion of the 100-yard sprints, 18 included the 50-yard sprints, 23 included either the 440-yard run, 880-yard run or the mile run, and 9 used either the 60-yard, 80-yard or 120-yard low hurdles in their schedule. Fifteen respondents included two types of running out of the three types, namely sprints, jogs, and hurdles, 11 respondents included all three, and 10 included just one of the three.

It was concluded that, as 92.3 per cent of the respondents utilized running or hurdling in the pre-season period, they are of value to the javelin thrower in his conditioning program. Despite variation of the running schedules, among the 36 respondents 26 included at least two types of runs in the schedules.

General Activity. Thirty respondents participated in stretching exercises, 27 in flexibility exercises, 12 in gymnastics, 12 in swimming, and these were considered as beneficial to general conditioning for javelin throwing. It is concluded that general physical activity aids in the coordination of flexibility of the body and this can be considered as beneficial to javelin throwing.

Hard Throwing. Twenty of the 24 throwers practiced with throws of over 200 feet, and 11 of the 15 coaches advised hard throwing during the pre-season training period. It is concluded by this number of respondents, which is 79.5 per cent of the total, that hard throwing is recommended even in pre-season practice.

Special Exercises. Twenty-eight of the combined coaches and throwers utilized special exercises structured for a javelin thrower. Pulling a javelin connected to a cable with a weight attached, a fixed rope with a javelin grip attached, a medicine ball throw, a weighted javelin throw, exercises with a shot, wall pulley exercises, and flexion exercises were among special exercises mentioned. It is concluded that, analogous to the weight program previously discussed, the special exercise portion of the pre-season training program is also individualized. It is implied that specially devised exercises for the javelin thrower may be worth consideration in developing muscles and coordination in movements which are used primarily in the javelin throw.

Javelin Technique Practice. Twenty-seven respondents included javelin technique practice in the pre-season training schedule. The approach run, the throwing position, the release and recovery, and the withdrawal and cross over received the greatest amount of practice time, in that order. It is concluded that pre-season practice of these techniques is advantageous to good throwing.

General Pre-Season Training Schedule. Two throwers included workouts on the pre-season training schedule every day of the week. Nineteen included six days a week for practice sessions and 8 included five days a week. Twenty-eight respondents practiced from 60 to 90 minutes each day on the average but the tendency was for longer sessions on alternate days with shorter sessions in between. It is concluded that an average of one to one and one-half hours a day, five or six days a week, is utilized for pre-season training training practice in the javelin throw.

IN-SEASON TRAINING

Weight Training. Twenty-nine respondents participated in a weight-lifting program in-season as compared to 34 respondents who lifted weights during the pre-season training period. The most used exercises were half-squats, bent arm pull-overs, bench presses, straight arm pull-overs, curls and sit-ups, listed in the order of their popularity. The in-season weight training schedule was shortened from that used in pre-season by 16 of the 28 utilizing weight-lifting. The methods used to shorten the weight training program were decreasing the number of days in the week lifting was done, doing fewer repetitions, doing fewer exercises, reducing the amount of weight lifted or continuing the program for only part of the competitive season.

From this it can be concluded that, while not as many throwers and coaches utilized a weight training program during the competitive season as did pre-season, it is of value to the physical condition of the thrower for 74.4 per cent of the respondents did recommend it. The majority of those using the program shortened it for the competitive season which leads to the conclusion that is it preferable to lift weight less strenuously in-season.

Increase or Decrease of Weight Lifted. Among the 29 respondents recommending a weight training program during the in-season, 8 increased the amount of weight lifted as the season progressed, 12 decreased the amount of weight and 9 kept the amount the same as it was pre-season. There is no apparent conclusion as to the increase or decrease of weight lifted as the season progresses.

Isometric Program. Only 3 respondents indicated the use of isometric exercises during the competitive season. From this it can be concluded that javelin throwers use other than an isometric program of training for the javelin throw.

Hard Throwing. Thirty-four respondents recommended making practice throws of over 210 feet. Most of the hard throwing was done on Mondays, Tuesdays, or Wednesdays, but usually not on all three days by the same thrower. The respondents indicated a wide range in the number of hard throws in practice, extending from as few as 3 to as many as 60 in one practice session. The average number of practice throws on one day among only the throwers was 19 in the early part of the week and 8 in the latter part of the week. The average number of hard practice throws advocated by the coaches was less than by the throwers, with 10 the average number of hard practice throws recommended by coaches in the early part of the week and from 3 to 4 in the latter part of the week.

Since 87.2 per cent of the combined coaches and throwers advocated throwing in practice, it can be concluded that it is a highly commendable method of training for improving throwing ability. It is also concluded that the throwers on the average take more hard throws in practice than the coaches recommend.

Javelin Technique Practice. Thirty-eight of the 39 respondents advocated technique practice during the competitive season. The throwing position and the approach run were the most extensively practiced, followed by the withdrawal and the release and recovery. Ten to 30 minutes comprised the average time spent on each technique. The implication is that due to the majority of respondents participating in technique practice in-season, it is a very valuable part of the training program but the amount of time spent on each technique will be determined by the thrower, and will probably change from time to time.

Running Program. Nineteen sprinted the 100-yard dash, 16 sprinted the 50-yard dash, 11 jogged the mile, and 9 ran both the 440- and 880-yard runs as a part of the in-season training program. The total number utilizing some type of running in the competitive season was 35, which implies that running is also an important activity in the in-season training program.

Warming-Up Exercises. Thirty-eight respondents advocated stretching or flexibility exercises during the warm-up period prior to throwing, and from 15 to 20 minutes comprised the average time spent. It is concluded that stretching or flexibility exercises are an important part of the warm-up period for most javelin throwers.

Practice Time. The throwers averaged five and one-half hours of practice time a week in-season and the coaches suggested an average of just under five hours. Of the combined coaches and throwers, 22 favored five practices a week and 10 advised practices six days a week. It is concluded that as over three-quarters of the respondents practice five or more days a week during the competitive season, this is desirable for a thrower to keep himself in the best physical condition.

OFF-SEASON ACTIVITIES

During that time of the year when no special training for the javelin event is maintained, an athlete will usually participate in at least one or more other physical activities. When extra-curricular physical activities were rated by the respondents as potential aids in sustaining their good throwing condition, weight-lifting received the highest rating, followed by weight-throwing, swimming, and gymnastics. It is concluded that any physical activity which promotes strength, endurance, flexibility, and coordination can be considered as a constructive activity.

In summary, the study would support these recommendations:

Pre-Season

- Ideally the javelin thrower should spend from four to six months on a pre-season training program, emphasizing overall body conditioning.
- Weight training should be a vital part of the conditioning program with an emphasis on body strength during the pre-season period.
- Running, preferably both sprints and jogs, should be included in the training schedule.
- Javelin technique practice should be an important aspect of the training program with the inclusion of hard throwing practice.
- Specially devised exercises for the javelin thrower are highly recommended.
- For the best results, a javelin thrower should work out from one to one and one-half hours a day, five or six days a week during the pre-season training period.

In-Season

- Weight training should be utilized during the competitive season, but to a lesser degree than pre-season, and should emphasize speed and endurance.
- Javelin techniques should definitely be practiced in-season, along with hard throwing practice.
- Running should be included in the schedule of training for the in-season period.

- Fifteen to 20 minutes should be used for a thorough warming-up period prior to hard throwing, with flexibility and stretching exercises included in the warm-up.
- Five or more practices a week, with an average total time of five and one-half hours, should be held in-season.

Off Season

A javelin thrower should participate in physical activities which promote strength, endurance, flexibility, and coordination during that part of the year when no special work is done in preparation for the javelin event.

Recommendations for Coaches

- A coach should be flexible when teaching javelin techniques and when planning training schedules for the throwers.
- A coach should avoid involving a thrower with too many coaching techniques for fear of overcoaching.

Recommended Research

- A study should be made which compares the javelin techniques utilized by the best 15 United States javelin throwers and the 15 best javelin throwers in the world.
- A study should be made on the psychological aspects of throwing the javelin.
- A study should be made to determine the cause of elbow injuries of javelin throwers and a means of prevention.

16

RESISTANCE EXERCISE TAILORED TO FIT THE JAVELIN THROWER

Dr. Arthur L. Dickinson
Arizona State University

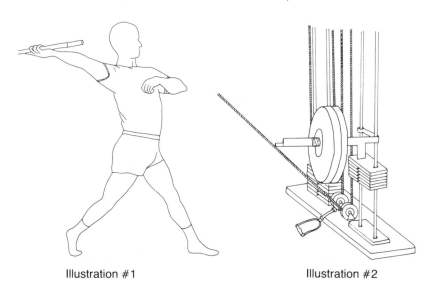

Illustration #1   Illustration #2

While resistance exercise has been employed to improve performance in many track and field events, participants in the javelin throw have either used it very little, or have been neither vocal nor literal in describing their routines. Perhaps this has been due to the difficulty of exercising the primary muscles of propulsion in a position similar to that of a throwing motion, or to a conviction that throwing a one and three-quarter pound object needs little oomph to propel it anyway.

Be that as it may, in cooperation with Frank Covelli (1963 West Coast Relays, Compton Relays, and NCAA Champion with a best mark of 264 feet) and Jon Cole, a fine freshman weight man, we developed a resistance exercise apparatus for the javelin thrower which seemed to show enough promising results to warrant offering the idea to others.

The basic exercise apparatus was a wall pulley-weight in which the original cotton cordage was replaced by three-eighths inch nylon rope. Above the weight pan, a one-inch diameter iron bar was welded as described by Klein[1], (Illustration 1), so that any desired weight of barbell plating could be added to augment the weights of the apparatus.

In order that a reasonable facsimile of throwing form could be executed against resistance, a two-foot portion of a javelin shaft including the whipping was rescued from a stack of broken equipment, and to it was securely fastened a twelve-inch loop of belt webbing. Thus, to use the pulley-weight apparatus as a resistance exercise for the javelin thrower, the pulley handle was merely unhooked, the belt webbing looped over the now bare hook, and resistance exercise performed which closely duplicated the form used in the javelin throw (Illustration 2). This emphasis upon the similarity of the exercise to the event where improvement is desired is based on a study by Rasch[2], who found that strength increases of a muscle exercised in one position did not necessarily carry over to the same muscle exercised in a different position.

Frank Covelli exercised in this manner not only in his pre-season conditioning program, but throughout his entire competitive period. At times he relied on this routine for his primary workout prior to an important meet, and we believe this apparatus may have been a contributing factor to his markedly improved performance from the previous season, when his best effort yielded a distance of only two hundred and thirty-two feet.

The exact amount of benefit to javelin throwers from performing pulley-weight exercises can never be measured objectively. However, that it is in all likelihood helpful is further suggested from a study by Railey[3], in which a group of ten Arizona State baseball players improved in baseball throwing velocities by amounts ranging from one to seven miles per hour following an eight-week training program that utilized the wall pulley-weight apparatus to perform a simulated baseball throw against resistance.

Certainly we have been sufficiently impressed with the possibilities of this apparatus to recommend its inclusion in the training programs for shot and discus performers, competitive swimmers, baseball pitchers.

References

1. Klein, Karl K. "Increasing the Functional Use of the Pulley-Weight Apparatus for Progressive Resistance Exercise," Journal of the National Athletic Trainers Association, II, (June, 1958).

2. Rasch, Philip J. and Laurence E Morehouse. "Effect of Static and Dynamic Exercises on Muscular Strength and Hypertrophy," Journal of Applied Physiology, XI (July, 1957).

3. Railey, James H. "The Effects of Two Methods of Resistance Exercise on Baseball Throwing Velocity." Unpublished Study; Tempe, Arizona, Arizona State University.

17

THE HAMMER THROW

Doug Raymond
Kent State University

Many times we have been asked what we have been doing differently in our coaching as compared to the methods employed by other coaches in this event. We will try to describe our method in a manner that will be understandable and applicable in helping develop 200-foot plus throwers.

Al Schoterman and Jacques Accambray not only erased the existing NCAA 35-pound weight and 16-pound hammer records, but did so with convincing authority. They became known as the awesome duo after 68 feet, 10 inches, and 67 feet, 7½ inches in the NCAA 35-pound weight championship. Outdoors their efforts produced 227 feet, 10½ inches and 224 feet, 6 inches placing them 2, 3 in the AAU hammer and 2, 4 in the 35-pound weight events.

Al Schoterman came to Kent State with a discus background and a best of 171 feet with the high school discus. In addition, he had a background of weight training that he started when he was 9 years old to build himself up due to a rheumatic condition. During his freshman year he limited his action to the shot and discus because of a lower back strain caused by throwing the javelin. At the beginning of his sophomore year, we started him on the hammer and his progress was rapid in that he had developed excellent balance and sound skill training from his competition in the discus. In the 35-pound weight event, he was even more remarkable, attaining 50-foot throws after only three weeks of throwing and a best of 63 feet, 1½ inches after only one season of throwing. He failed to qualify for the finals in the NCAA 35-pound event as a sophomore after suffering a bad case of influenza.

The Hammer Throw

Jacques Accambray matriculated at Kent State University from France when he was only 19 years old. As a 15-year-old he threw the 12-pound hammer 184 feet, and 170 feet with the international 16-pound hammer. As a 17-year-old, he threw the 12-pound hammer 209 feet and the 16-pound hammer 193 feet. One year later he set a world junior record of 233 feet, 3½ inches with the 16-pound hammer. Jacques had a sensational year as a freshman with both the 35-pound weight and the 16-pound hammer. His best was 67 feet, 7½ inches with the 35-pound weight and 227 feet, 10½ inches with the 16-pound hammer for a runner-up position to his teammate, Schoterman, in the 35-pound weight and the second best by a collegian and a best at the outdoor NCAA by a collegian.

Jacques had been beautifully trained by Henri Vasseur, who is the regional technical coach for northern France, and William Fourreau, the national field events coach of France. Both had spent a great deal of time perfecting his style. We might mention that Jacques' 227 feet, 10½ inches is also a French national record making him a leading contender for a hammer throwing berth on the French Olympic team in Munich this summer.

Jacques and Al hit it off right away and are fast friends, always working out together. Their styles are different in that Jack starts much faster and closely approximates the style of the European greats, while Al starts out slowly on his first turn and has a gradual build-up doing the final with a ferocity much like Bondarchuk, the fine Russian thrower and former world record holder.

Too many coaches take too much for granted and fail to emphasise the assets which are essential for championship competitive efforts. It is imperative that the athlete know something about the history of the event. Also, the importance of a sound program in weight training should be emphasized. This includes the equipment available for use at the practice sessions. This equipment should include Olympic size barbells (400-pound sets) at least two, bench press machines, leg lift machine, incline boards, chinning bar, dumbbells 25 pounds through 100 pounds, squat racks, and power rack. We have a large dressing room and this equipment is located within this area for the exclusive use of our athletes. We also have another complete weight room which contains two Universal Gyms which are valuable because many exercises can be done by hooking up the handles for arm pulls, overhead pulls, lat pulls, etc. Track men should also be aware of the equipment needed (gloves), how to install wires, add weight to hammers, the care of equipment, and the safety aspects involved.

Al Schoterman started to learn the event by using the 35-pound weight. He had the necessary strength. Quicker results can be obtained with the 35-pound weight over the 16-pound hammer in that more mistakes can be made and still the athlete is able to get it off. The action is slower which fits into a beginner's way of doing things, and with this in mind he should learn

In learning a pivot turn, the thrower in slow motion should go into a preliminary turn.

the fundamental of throwing. We have a 20-, 25- or 28-pound weight made to be used during the learning process, being sure to go from 16 to 20, to 25, 28 and then 35.

We suggest building a cement platform 10 feet wide by 20 feet long, pulling out the surface fairly smooth so that practice turns can be executed. I have found that by using an ordinary broom in place of the hammer the athlete learns the turns quite readily. The preliminary turn should be kept well back to the right side of the athlete's body with the back of the hands passing over and slightly beyond the top of the head. At the low point, the hands, if they are extended, should not go below the thrower's waist. Numerous practice sessions must be spent developing a sound preliminary turn in order to feel the importance of counterbalance, balance, and rhythm which are necessary in this event. In this action, the athlete must learn to use hip acion or rotation which imparts more speed to the ball.

In learning a pivot turn, the thrower in slow motion should go into a preliminary turn. Upon completing two turns and as soon as the hammer approaches his right foot in its plane around the body, he should pivot on his left heel approximately 180 degrees, keeping his hands no higher than shoulder level and his right knee back. This latter move is necessary in that most American throwers allow the right knee to tuck behind the left knee and leg, thus decreasing ball radius but increasing body speed which upsets balance and counterbalance. Several other factors must also be taken into consideration and the thrower should realize that he has but one axis, his left leg and foot. The right leg is nothing more than a stabilizer. The push off the right leg, upon a completed turn, increases speed and, when timed with the release driving straight upward in a vertical plane, increases throwing lift or distance.

In the beginning, we instruct the thrower to keep his right foot anchored until the ball has traveled slightly more than 90 degrees and his left foot is approximately 180 degrees. Then he should drive off it, being sure to keep the weight of his body over the left leg or axis. He should turn quickly to the beginning position but some 1½ feet straight down the circle diameter, picking off the hammer as it comes into the 280 degree point or approximately 30 degrees farther back from the point the first turn was started. The thrower is trying to beat the ball around and can practice this many times without the hammer in slow motion and later with the hammer. Prior to going into any turn, the knees must be slightly flexed at first for beginners and, as they gain throwing technique, they should be bent more. The back should always be kept straight.

After a thrower has a reasonable knowledge of the pivot turn and displays good balance and counterbalance, completing each turn with his shoulders parallel to the ground, a straight back, arms extended, and hands even with the hip extended, have him go into a slow first pivot turn. Then have him go into a faster second and a still faster third pivot turn, rest, and repeat until it becomes a habit.

In order to have a good release, the athlete must have a sound knowledge of how a hammer thrower develops centrifugal force to impart ball velocity and how to utilize this velocity in order to get distance on the throw. Let us suppose we are skating and all of a sudden someone yells "Let's form a whip." One person becomes the pivot man and he describes a circle fairly wide at first, but then as the skaters join the line he pivots in a tighter and tighter arc, making it more and more difficult for the skaters to join. Often the last skaters break off due to the tremendous centrifugal pull outward or they deliberately do so, with the resulting action of flying down the ice at a great rate of speed. Hammer throwing closely resembles this action with a few exceptions; the thrower must stay within a 7-foot circle, perform off a cement circle, not ice, and use throwing shoes with semi-hard rubber soles in place of skates.

The Hammer Throw

To pick up ball velocity, a thrower must always keep his arms fully extended except when the ball is picked off behind his right shoulder and then his right arm shortens slightly. He should learn to tighten his turns, especially the second and third. He must try to maintain a good plane and for the release must get a full three-quarters turn pull by picking off the ball behind his right shoulder. Now he should pull hard on the hammer while his leg drives directly upward. This pulling movement produces height, extra distance, and helps prevent fouling in that the thrower is driving upward and not outward.

Facts to Remember:
- Practice turns as often as possible using the broom and the hammer. Do as many as 4 or 5 at first and later 8 to 10.
- Keep the right knee back prior to going into a turn in order to ensure a long radius and get more torque on the waist, which in turn gives added ball velocity each time torque is released.
- Do not allow a high plane. Keep the hands at shoulder level when one-quarter through the turn and slightly above shoulder level when the ball is directly behind or 180 degrees.
- Practice on turn releases. Our throwers wind up with two or three preliminary turns. Then they go into an all-out single turn and release keeping track of distance. Jacques Accambray does 185 feet and Al Schoterman the same.
- Use weight training because it is the quickest way to develop the needed strength for this event.
- About two weeks prior to the start of the meets slack off on heavy weights, but continue with the lighter ones, using fast repetitions to speed up muscle action.

Part 2
The
Horizontal
Jumps

18
TIPS FOR A LONG JUMP

Bob Epskamp
Ohio State University

A world record that lasted a long time was Jesse Owens' long jump of 26 feet, 8¼ inches established in 1935. At the present time, Ralph Boston has a pending mark for world recognition of 27 feet, 5 inches.

Jesse Owens was an outstanding sprinter and hurdler as well as a long jumper and held world records in the 100, 200 low hurdles, and long jump all at the same time. Ralph Boston is an excellent hurdler and better than average high jumper.

The world's top long jumpers have been outstanding sprinters and this is no coincidence. However, long jumpers without outstanding sprinting ability may become top performers if they specialize in the event and perfect all of the details of technique.

Let us list some of the areas to be considered for the long jump. They are:

- The approach.
- Take-off.
- Action in the air.
- Landing.

THE APPROACH

From the very first strides, the approach should be an accumulation of speed. One of the most neglected phases of jumping is the failure to consider the first strides on the jumper's approach and what they mean to his actual effort.

The approach depends upon a consistent, hard, relaxed start. If the jumper is to take off from his left foot, he should begin his approach by stepping first with his left foot and having his check marks on the left side of the runway.

Research studies have shown that athletes never reach maximum speed until after they have passed 40 yards; therefore, for first-class performance an athlete should have an approach of 125 feet or over.

Regardless of the length of the run, at least two check marks should be used. The athlete should stand on his mark at the head of the runway and start hard and relaxed in the same manner each time. The second check mark should be placed approximately 60 feet from the take-off board and is merely a green light when the runner passes this mark, concentrating on maximum speed on his run.

For the individual who consistently arrives beyond the take-off board, the coach should move both check marks back the same distance until the right distance has been obtained. Runway surface conditions and wind velocity will cause changes in check marks. However, once the steps have been accurately determined and measured, the athlete should not run through or jump without having a complete warm-up and his steps measured with a steel tape measure.

One of the most common faults among novice long jumpers is looking down at a take-off board. It is extremely important that the habit of looking down at the board not be developed for it destroys mental concentration of running off the board and a long jump.

Once the athlete is sure of his check marks, then he can concentrate on obtaining maximum relaxed speed. Confidence in the approach is very important and can only be gained through a minimum of change.

During the last three or four strides, the trunk should be brought upright, the hips slightly lowered so the powerful extensor muscles of the legs are in an excellent position for a vigorous, explosive, take-off. It is important to accomplish these points with little loss of speed, because speed and spring together give the jumper the long jump.

A jumper should also change his mental concentration from speed to actual jumping. The presence of any doubt about hitting the board correctly will destroy his mental concentration on jumping.

THE TAKE-OFF

The take-off foot should come to the board in advance of the body, with the take-off foot partially flexed. As the body passes quickly over the take-off foot, the leg should extend powerfully and the foot should complete a heel-ball-toe action.

At the same time the free leg should be swept forward and upward quickly and powerfully to assist in lift at take-off. The jumper should experience a feeling of running off the board.

From the time the rock-up action of the take-off foot starts, the athlete must concentrate his effort, driving his chin, chest, and eyes as high into the air as possible.

The actual forward-upward lift off the board must be made in a split second to conserve the forward speed gained by the accumulation of speed in the approach. This high-speed action must be practiced in order to be executed effectively.

Many coaches have their jumpers spend countless hours taking pop-ups using a fast 50-foot run. This running off the board action, when done so many times with a short non-fatiguing run, becomes mechanical and generally is executed perfectly when a full run is used in competition.

ACTION IN THE AIR

The form used in the air is for balance and is an effort to get the feet in position for landing. Most authorities agree that the hitch-kick style is the best type of mid-air movement, and when performed efficiently, enables the athlete to land with his feet slightly in advance of his flight path of center of gravity than is the case with the hang or sail styles. Both Ralph Boston and Igor Ter-Ovanesyan use the hitch-kick in the long jump.

Because of the hitch-kick the jumper arrives in a landing position with his trunk near the upright position. During the flight the arms should work in conjunction with the legs in a windmill type action. The legs should be in a continuous motion forward during the jump.

At the point of take-off for a left-footed jumper, the left arm should go out, come back to the body, and then go in a reverse windmill action. Simultaneously, the right arm should stay close to the body at take-off, then move up toward the head, be dropped down, and then go in a reverse windmill.

LANDING

Landing provides the finishing touch to the long jump. In a well-timed landing, the buttocks are but a fraction of an inch above the level of the ex-, tended heels as they touch the ground. Oftentimes the jumper will sit down in the pit; however, at least the coach is aware that he has his feet out in front of his body.

Landing requires as much work as take-off and can be accomplished with pop-ups. In landing, the feet should be spread not more than 10 inches apart. The knees should bend. The arms should swing downward and back and just at landing should be driven forward to assist in the rock over the heels.

As outstanding sprinters specialize more and more in the long jump, certainly the 28-foot long jump will be accomplished in the near future.

Landing requires as much work as the take-off.

19

STYLE IN THE LONG JUMP

Ted Runner
University of Redlands

Jerry Proctor has outstanding athletic ability. He is an excellent hurdler, 14.0, and runs the 100 in 9.4. If he is to continue to improve in the long jump, he must use more natural speed on the long jump runway. At the same time he must be able to develop a take-off position at the board relative to his use of increased speed. He has had problems with scratching, and this tends to make him a cautious jumper instead of one who jumps with confidence. He is gradually overcoming this, and if he continues to use more of his natural speed, with control, he may come close to Beamon's phenomenal mark of 29 feet, 2½ inches.

Illustration 1 shows Proctor just prior to his left foot hitting the runway one stride from his take-off. He is running tall with his head and attention up preparing for his last stride before take-off.

In Illustration 2, Jerry is shown on his last stride before take-off. He is lowering his center of gravity prior to raising it at the take-off board. This enables him to get the good height that he attains. He is looking up and thinking up.

Illustration 3 shows Proctor moving forward and up with his center of gravity along the line of movement at the take-off board.

As shown in Illustration 4, Jerry's center of gravity has just passed the vertical plane through the foot on the ground. He is pushing and pawing against the take-off board with all his might as his swing through leg is moving ahead and swinging forward to begin his first stride.

Illustrations 5, 6, and 7 show Jerry continuing his first stride and beginning his second stride. Nothing special may be said except that he is inclined to be a little too stiff and does not get the loose running through the air that is characteristic of Boston's style. Boston takes three strides in the air whereas Jerry is taking two. As Proctor continues to develop, he will probably use the three-stride jump technique. He will overcome his stiffness in the air, which should result in better balance and control.

Illustrations 8, 9, and 10 show Jerry's left leg coming up to join the right, and his trunk and arms coming forward and down as a counterbalance. In Illustration 10, notice that the left leg has been brought through and past the right leg. Jerry actually has a tendency to drop his right leg at this point, probably due to the long time he has to keep it up.

Jerry makes an efficient landing enabling him to end up with a fine mark of 26 feet, 11 ¾ inches (Illustrations 11 and 12).

The world's top long jumpers have been outstanding sprinters.

20

LONG JUMP *OR* TRIPLE JUMP

By
John E. Nulton
Foothill College

The long and triple jump are both running and jumping events. They have more basic similarities than differences in terms of physical requirements, performance skills, and training techniques. Therefore, it is logical and reasonable to expect the athlete who performs well in one to double in the other. A good jumping prospect should be required to practice and jump in both of these events. The previous statement is right? No, it is wrong.

Looking around at high school and junior college competition in these two jumping events would certainly lead one to suspect that the plausible logic stated previously has been accepted by many coaches. It is quite obvious that the practice of doubling in the long and triple jump is commonly encouraged or tolerated. Perhaps the pressure of striving to accumulate team points in order to succeed in dual meet competition has played a part in utilizing good jumping potential in both events. Whatever the underlying rationale or motivation, this unfortunate practice is common.

Long Jump or Triple Jump

Jumping in one form or another, is one of the oldest athletic events. Some form of the long and triple jump has been performed since the ancient Greek Olympiads, and perhaps before. Both events are well know in national and international competition. The long jump has been a part of high school and collegiate track and field for many years. The triple jump, while a rather new event on some levels and in many areas, is growing in popularity. Although most coaches have an understanding of the basics of the long jump, they have had little or no exposure to the triple jump, either as competitors or teachers. We feel this is an important contributing factor to the presence of the common doubling practice. An individual is found who demonstrates interest or potential in the long jump. Since the triple jump is an event on the track schedule, he is expected to include this event in his program. We are led to conclude from our observations that the long jump is treated by most coaches as something the individual does naturally. Most jumpers we have observed from high school through junior college appear to be somewhat inadequately coached in technique and not conditioned for the tremendous physical demands required in the execution of the jump. Most long jumpers perform is such a way that they encourage one to surmise that long jumping has been looked upon by their coach as something they do in addition to some other more well-coached event.

The triple jump is probably the most poorly executed track event found today. We feel that this results from the event being the most poorly coached event at the present time. Certainly the great majority of the athletes we have observed performing in the triple jump event exhibit either a fundamentally inaccurate understanding of the elements involved, a poorly coached or seldom practiced event, or an inappropriately trained and conditioned body. This is a tremendously challenging event and it is indeed unfortunate to find so few athletes performing it well.

It is important that both the coach and athlete grasp the fact that the long jump and the triple jump are separate and distinct events requiring a different psychological orientation and physical expression. Both demand specific training programs. Both require practice, practice, and more practice. The very nature of these two jumping events requires tremendous emphasis and that strains be placed upon the jumping feet, ankles, and knees, as well as upon the lower back. Both events are what must be considered high injury risk activities. The long jump and triple jump are fundamentally similar only in the extensive pounding experienced and the general abuse inflicted upon the jumper's heels, ankles, and knees.

Heel bruises are commonly associated with both jumping events. These may involve a breakdown of the fibrous fatty heel pad and/or injury to the calcaneal tuberosity. While the heel pad is adequate to absorb occasional jumping, unusual or continued trauma leads to its breakdown. Once they

It is important for coaches and athletes to understand that the long jump and the triple jump are separate and distinct events requiring a different psychological orientation and physical expression.

occur, such injuries heal slowly, are extremely painful, and crippling. Jumping on tender heels results in uncontrollable postural adjustment in both running and jumping. This, in turn, increases the chances of strains, sprains, and other injuries. The running and jumping required in training and performance of these events is unusually demanding of the structures of the heel. If the athlete is required or expected to perform in both events, the wear and tear on the heels is tremendous, increasing the possibility of breakdown. While improved performance skills will reduce the individual smacking effect of each contact with the ground, repetition and practice will not strengthen the heel pad or condition it to withstand greater punishment. Work that involves heel pounding must be carefully selected and limited. If the athlete is to perfect the necessary skills in both the long jump and triple jump, and achieve the level of physical conditioning required to excel, the exercises and drills used will make this impossible.

Sprained ankles and sprained and strained arches occur frequently. We have observed these injuries more often in athletes who are doubling. Our experience has shown that their occurrence is often associated wit the execution of a portion of one of the events in which there has been an inability to adjust a parallel, yet different skill (i.e. following several long jumps, taking off into the triple jump too high, overleaning, and landing upon the runway off-balance). A jumper with a weakened or limited ankle or foot will not be able to develop the proper heel-toe rocking technique so necessary to a powerful first effort in either event. A taped ankle cannot extend well and will fail to exert that final lifting effort so essential in both the long and triple jump.

Shin splints, Achilles tendon strains, hamstring pulls, and low back pain are all found among long and triple jumpers. While adequate conditioning and skill improvement reduce the chances of developing these problems, excessive work requirements placed upon these areas will increase the possibility of their occurrence. We have seen several jumpers turn up lame with one or another of these problems where the only observable cause was excessive muscle use and fatigue. These injuries are often identified in athletes who are otherwise well trained and conditioned, and who have performed proper warm-up and stretching activities. Overwork, insufficient variety, and fatigue are most often the culprits. If the athlete is going to have a chance to achieve success in these two events by doubling, it will be impossible to avoid the dangers without seriously handicapping his training program. It is indeed disheartening for the athlete and coach to have the injuries and ailments previously mentioned destroy a well-planned and well-executed pre-season conditioning program. Placing the serious conscientious athlete in two equally demanding events, stacks the deck against him. We feel the odds are not worth the gamble. Doubling in the long and triple jump is a fool's bet.

Let us take a brief look at the first two fundamentals associated with both the long jump and triple jump, the approach run and the take-off. Regardless of the obvious differences in the other fundamental skills found in the approach runs of the two events are the most overlooked and misunderstood.

In the long jump, the running speed and the approach run length are entirely dependent upon the jumper's ability to convert his maximum obtainable forward velocity into instant upward and outward driving power from the take-off board. If he is exceptionally fast and can accelerate rapidly, his approach run distance can be relatively short. Distances of from 80 to 90 feet, though not uncommon in use, are generally too short for effective long jumping. Short runs result in complete acceleration at the board, forward overbalancing, and a jumping out action. Sensible starting distances will be found somewhere between 100 to 115 feet. As the jumper becomes able to handle his potential speed, and develops leg strength and power, even greater lengths can be utilized. Outstanding long jumpers usually achieve optimum off-the-board conditions with an approach run that requires around 17 to 19 strides.

The long jumper's approach run should resemble a sprinter running the 50-yard dash. As he drives down the runway, he must strive to achieve his maximum convertible running speed. He must condition himself psychologically to run while thinking *UP*.

During the last five strides, the long jumper must prepare himself for the take-off. This requires an adjustment in both stride length and body and head position. The first three of the last five must be lengthened slightly in order that the jumper will be able to lower his center of gravity, thereby coiling the spring for the take-off. He must also try to get his knees a bit higher and his arms a bit lower in order to facilitate relaxation and balance. His forward running body lean should be corrected so that he will be running upright during his last two strides to the board. During this stride adjustment, or settling, as well as during the following gather, there must be no slowing down of running speed. The jumper's last two strides should be somewhat shorter, 6 to 12 inches shorter, than the three preceding strides, and his knees should be bent slightly. His head should rock backward enabling him to look as well as think *UP*. These final adjustments will facilitate the upward explosion from the board and will transfer the jumper's center of gravity slightly backward, thus developing a better take-off angle for the upward drive. His arms must be prepared to drive forcefully upward from the take-off to assist in the endeavor to achieve maximum height.

In the triple jump, running speed and approach run length are predicated upon the jumper's ability to control effectively his built-up forward velocity while achieving an even, consistent, balanced, coordinated, and rhythmic running style. He must be able to run through the take-off board without an appreciable loss of momentum. He must prepare psychologically for three consecutive forward, outward, and upward lifts.

It is common to see young, inexperienced triple jumpers utilizing approach running distances associated with the long jump. This results in an inability to achieve a consistent running stride, to develop a controlled, balanced, and rhythmic running style, and to utilize available running speed. It will also tend to make it difficult for the jumper to stay low on his first effort.

A good starting distance for a triple jumper's approach run will be somewhere between 115 to 125 feet. As he achieves control and stride consistency, he can increase the length of his run to accommodate his maximum usable speed. Outstanding triple jumpers require between 21 to 23 strides to develop optimal take-off board performance.

As the triple jumper strides down the runway, he must strive to achieve a relaxed, full stride. The split of his legs must be as wide as he can control. As he strides toward the board, he must be thinking *through*. He must avoid striving for speeds greater than he can control. His running strides should appear similar to those of a low hurdler or pole vaulter. He must approach the take-off board with a full, relaxed running style. His stride must be consistent throughout. No settling or gathering should be attempted. Rhythm, consistency, and balance are important. The triple jumper must do everything possible to avoid losing the forward velocity he has built up throughout his approach run. He must leave the take-off board conserving his forward momentum. He should reach the board with his upper body canted slightly forward. His chest must be up and his head should be in good center alignment, resting upon his shoulders. He should be looking forward or toward his hip landing position. He should have an approach run long enough for him to achieve his functional running speed several strides out from the take-off board, thereby enabling him to arrive at the board with a relaxed, controlled running stride. His arms should be assisting in maintaining his balance.

Is there still any doubt that there are basic, critical differences between the way in which the long jump and triple jump begin?

Now, let us examine the long jump and triple jump take-off. The differences here are fundamental and critical to the successful completion of each event. It has been our experience that the occurrence of injuries to athletes doubling in these two events during competition stems from an inability to convert successfully from one technique to the other. The good long jumper who competes in the triple jump will often bound up and out during his triple jump efforts, landing hard and off-balance on his heel as he completes his hop. The triple jumper, doubling in the long jump, jumps out, into the pit, driving his heels hard into the sand, often resulting in sprained ankles. It is rare to witness a doubler who is equally proficient in both types of take-off with any degree of consistency during a meet.

The long jumper must arrive at the take-off board thinking and acting *UP*. Examine diagrams 1-4 of outstanding long jumpers. Can there be any doubt that on taking off from the board, these athletes were *UP* oriented?

The long jumper has developed his maximum usable horizontal speed, which he must strive to convert into the highest vertical lift possible. Although he has made stride adjustments just before the board, he must endeavor to get to the board without speed reduction. His foot plant and action must be a fast heel-toe rocker method, yet he must strive to remain in contact with the board as long as possible in order to pull, push, and extend *UP*. In other words, he must make maximum use of the board during his brief contact with it. As the heel of his jump leg reaches the board, his jump leg knee flexes slightly and his free leg swings forward from the hip, with the knee well flexed. At this point, directly over the board, the jumper's upper body must be vertical and he must be looking and thinking *UP*.

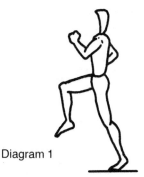

Diagram 1

Long Jump Take-Off Action
- Greg Bell -

Diagram 2

Long Jump Take-Off Action
- Jerry Proctor -

Diagram 3

Long Jump Take-Off Action
- Boston -

Diagram 4

Long Jump Take-Off Action
- Beamon -

With his center of gravity moving ahead of the board, the long jumper's jump leg must straighten powerfully, while the rocker action of the take-off foot is pulling and pushing at the board, culminating in an on-the-toes explosive ankle extension. Every effort must be exerted to get his upper body as high as possible. As this action is taking place, the jumper's free leg knee thrusts forward and up, assisting in the complete straightening of the jump leg knee and the upward driving of his torso.

As the long jumper leaves the board, he must striving to keep his upper body vertical, his chest forward, his head tilted back, and his chin and eyes *UP*. His arms must drive vigorously upward and his back must be arching. All efforts to achieve height must be imparted at the board. Nothing can be added to this objective once the jumper is in the air.

The triple jumper must arrive at the board thinking and acting *OUT*. Examine Diagrams 5-7 of the take-off action of these exceptional triple jumpers. Certainly it will be agreed that they present a picture of *OUT* orientation.

Diagram 5

Triple Jump Take-Off Action
- Schmidt (Poland) -

Diagram 6

Triple Jump Take-Off Action
- Kreer (U.S.S.R.) -

Diagram 7

Triple Jump Take-Off Action
- Saneyev (U.S.S.R.) -

As he takes off from the board, the triple jumper must strive to conserve a maximal amount of the controlled sprint speed he has developed. He must carry as much horizontal momentum through the take-off as possible. He wants to achieve forward movement through as long a hop as he can execute efficiently, with as low an upward lift as is feasible. He must maintain his running stride to and through the take-off board. His foot plant and action are also heel-to-toe, but with the foot rolling over, resulting in a smooth, shockless run-through take-off. He must develop a running-to-over-and-out take-off board action. He must avoid slamming his foot into the board or rocking back on his heel on take-off, because such actions decrease his forward momentum. He does not want to reach with his take-off foot for the board on his last stride because this will slow down his forward momentum.

The triple jumper wants his first effort to be balanced and controlled. This may require a slight checking of running speed at the board. His take-off foot must contact the board in advance of his center of gravity, but without a stretch. As his center of gravity moves forward, there is very little hip lowering and only a slight bending of the take-off leg and knee. Since his second take-off is from the same leg, he must adjust his body weight over his take-off leg just prior to his first take-off. During this forward movement his upper body is near vertical, with only a slight forward lean. As he takes off from the board, his body weight must be well balanced over his take-off leg but forward of his take-off foot. His take-off leg extension must be similar to that achieved by a powerful sprinter-hurdler. His take-off foot must be pulling him forward and outward from the board.

In order to facilitate his forward-outward effort, the triple jumper's free leg must be swung through quickly, flexed, and with the knee driven forward and upward vigorously to where the thigh is parallel to the ground. His arms should move alternately as do those of a sprinter, assisting in controlling his body balance. They must not be allowed to drop below his waist or swing back because this will result in a buckling of his landing leg.

The triple jumper must strive to maintain his head in normal body alignment. His eyes should be fixed straight ahead.

For this first phase of the triple jump, there is a critical and optimal take-off angle for each jumper which must be found. This requires considerable practice time, both in finding and perfecting its execution. It must be as low a take-off projection and flight trajectory as possible, considering individual running speed, leg strength, and general physique. If it is too low, the potential length of the hop will be reduced and the impact on landing will further reduce the forward momentum, as well as place great strain on the heel. It if is too high, the triple jumper's horizontal speed will be reduced, his landing will be hard, and his landing leg will likely buckle and collapse, resulting in a very short step phase.

We mentioned general physique as one of the considerations in the hop take-off. This brings us to our final point.

If coaches have the opportunity to select young candidates for either the long jump or triple jump, they should be careful and judicious. Do not start a boy working in an event for which he lacks certain vital, fundamental, and natural qualities that will be required if he is to have a reasonable chance of gaining success.

If a boy is going to be able to mature into a fine long jumper he must have great natural speed. He must certainly be at least an also ran competition quality sprinter. He must be able to achieve his maximum speed with rapid acceleration. Have the candidates run repeat 40's and look for quickness and a well-coordinated springy sprint stride. Observe carefully those boys who demonstrate determination and aggressiveness in their running efforts.

Look for natural spring and general overall body coordination. Does the candidate have resilience and spring in his stride?

Have the candidates perform several standing vertical and long jumps. Look for the boys who can execute powerful jumps in which they utilize quick, coordinated movements of their ankles, knees, and hips, assisted by effective back and arm action.

Any candidates who do poorly in either speed or spring screening should not be encouraged to continue training for the long jump.

Finally, does the candidate have sound, strong lower limbs? Does the physical appearance of his upper body and legs show good basic muscle' size? An adequate natural structural foundation must be present if the strength and stamina essential for successful long jumping are to be developed.

Successful triple jumpers have good speed, a fine sense of balance and coordination, a natural relaxed, stretch-stride running form, and exceptional resilient and springy muscles and joints in both legs. They are found to be in the middle body weight range, 165 to 175 pounds, and to represent the rather rangy, long-limbed tall body type.

Look for prospective triple jumpers among boys who aspire to being intermediate and high hurdlers or 440 and 880 runners. Select boys who, at physical maturity, will be a least 5 feet, 11 inches tall. The rather tall boy, 6 feet to around 6 feet, 2 inches, with the long thighs and calves is the ideal body type candidate. In addition, these candidates must have two strong and rugged legs as well as a strong back. Do not encourage a boy to participate in the triple jump who has a history of hip, knee, ankle, or foot troubles of the sprain-strain variety, or who has had a chronic lower back difficulty. The triple jump is a high injury risk event. It is no place for athletes with structurally weak or injury-prone legs.

Have the triple jump candidates run several repeat 60-yard sprints. Notice their acceleration striding pattern. Look for the boys who reach out on each

Successful triple jumpers have good speed, a fine sense of balance and coordination, a natural relaxed, stretch-stride running form, and exceptional resilient and springy muscles and joints in both legs.

stride and who run wide and loose. Be alert to those who exhibit ankle and leg resilience as they run. Make a record of those who display a natural smoothness, coordination, balance, and rhythm in their running style. Look for the candidates who run with upper body relaxation and natural arm swing.

Next, have the prospects perform several 20-yard high-knees, short stride runs (simple step-step drill). Instruct them to push off, up, and out with each foot and to lift their lead leg thigh as high as possible on each stride. Look for those boys who use a wide-crotch split-stride technique and who demonstrate good double leg power and ankle extension spring. Notice those boys who have the natural ability to utilize their upper body and arms effectively for balance, control, and stride lift.

Candidates who do poorly in these screening activities and/or do not measure up well on the physical qualities check list should not be considered for triple jump training.

Each year we see many college athletes competing in either the long jump or triple jump who are wrong for these events. Most of these jumpers have been participating in these event at least since high school. It is grossly unfair to encourage an athlete to strive to master the technical apsects of these events, and to undertake the rigorous conditioning and training required for success if, under even the best conditions, he can be expected to achieve an 18 foot, 5 inch to 19 foot, 6 inch long jump or a 38 foot, 6 inch to a 42 foot, 10 inch triple jump.

It is equally inappropriate to assume that because an athlete is capable of performing successfully in one of these events, he is suited to or capable of performing adequately in the other. Being able to withstand the strains and stresses of one jumping event does not qualify an athlete for survival in another.

We hope that this article has provided some useful information and some restraining influence on the subject of doubling in the long and triple jumps. It is also hoped that this presentation will cause coaches who work with athletes in these events to evaluate more carefully and critically the differences that exist. We have directed attention only to those that affect the initial effort. There are many more.

21
TRAINING FOR THE LONG JUMP AND TRIPLE JUMP DOUBLE

Hugh Hackett
University of New Mexico

Training for the long jump and the triple jump double should start in the fall. An athlete who wants to compete in this event cannot expect to attain top physical condition unless he is willing to follow a year-around program, and he will not be able to acquire the strength necessary in one year. The foundation is laid the first year. Then, each succeeding year physical strength is increased through training, and the strength and endurance which come with maturity build on this foundation. A few gifted athletes have the natural ability to long jump and triple jump in a few meets during early season. However, the requirements for competing a full season, consisting of seven or more meets, are intelligent physical preparation, definite supervision of practice and meet competition by a coach, and, of course, the athlete's desire to participate at his best.

Our workout program is broken down into four sections: September through December, January through February, March through June, and July through August. The following workout schedule is not detailed day by day, but it does point out our most important practice procedures.

The triple jump: Illustrations 1-10 illustrate the "hop" and the "step".

The triple jump: Illustrations 11-16 illustrate the "jump".

September through December

All workouts are based on a six-day week, Monday through Saturday. Three days a week, on alternate days, the track athletes run three to six miles of cross-country. This running is done on the golf course, taking advantage of rolling hills and grass running surface. There is no joy in cross-country running, particularly for a field event man. Therefore, the coach must do all he can to encourage the athlete to discipline himself mentally for this work. Running at first is slow and steady. After two weeks, fartlek, sprinting hills, jogging fairways, and any other type of distance training that can be incorporated are introduced. This type of running may make the workouts more varied and perhaps more enjoyable.

Three days a week, alternate days, are spent on weight training. Five weight training exercises are performed to retain or develop upper body strength. These exercises are the military press, bench press, bent arm pullovers, curls, and upright rowing. Two sets of seven repetitions are executed using quick arm action and a light load.

Our goal in weight training is the development of strength in the abdominal, lower back, hip, and leg areas. To achieve this end, the following exercises are used. Hang from a wall ladder, with the back flush against the wall, lift the legs simultaneously to a 90° position, and return to the hang position. Weights are added to the feet as strength increases. Back hyperextension, supine and prone, sit-ups, the knee raise, toe raise, and squat jump are also used. Three sets of seven repetitions are included in this set of exercises.

More effective strength exercises, which are performed at the stadium, include one-legged 50-yard hops, alternating legs each 50 yards, and the iron horse drill. This drill consists of a 130-pound I beam, cut so it pulls similar to a sled. The sled is connected to a belt placed around the athlete by a 10-foot piece of rope. It is pulled with digging, sprinter type steps, 25 yards six times, three days per week. We have two 130 pound I beams and one 160-pound I beam. We consider the iron horse our finest drill for this time of year.

January through February

Cross-country is continued twice each week. Weight training work remains the same as it was in the first phase. Emphasis on the importance of the runup is stressed during this period.

The first check mark or start of the run is marked with a hand limer. If the athlete takes off the board with his left foot, the hand limer is used again to mark each stride on the runway under the left foot all the way to the take-off board. There will be approximately twenty lime marks across the runway for a 125-foot run. This number, of course, will fluctuate, depending upon individual stride length. Repeated runway practice using these check marks will build confidence in the run, and give the athlete a sense of rhythm. Each track man uses the same length of run for the long jump and the triple jump. The rhythm, that is the actual feel of the run, is maintained, and rhythmic breathing is also stressed. Robinson exhales and inhales with each stride, loud enough to be noticeable, lets out a loud grunt as his take-off foot hits the board (or, in the case of the triple jump, grunts each time he hits the runway in the hop, step and jump).

It is important for the coach to be on the lookout for heel bruises during this phase of training. A heel cup, sponge rubber or shoes designed to protect the heel should be used. The practice runway should be composed of material that is soft enough to prevent heel bruises. If the runway is of very hard material, the athlete will lose the incentive needed for proper execution of the run. It is better for practice runways to be too soft rather than too hard, and in many instances the full run on grass alongside the actual runway is more effective for practice purposes. Speed, under control, is essential down the runway, and distance will increase in proportion to speed. A high knee action should be stressed. Height must be attained in the jump, but must be properly timed with action of the hitch kick to insure proper balance and landing. The jumper should have enough confidence in his step to permit the eyes to leave the take-off board 30 feet before hitting the board.

Our jumpers run 120-yards high hurdles on the grass for conditioning and rhythm of stride during this phase. If a boy cannot three step the college highs, the hurdles are moved to high school height; if he cannot make it over the high school height, they are moved to intermediate; and if he cannot make this height and three step, he will not be a successful long or triple jumper.

March through June

This is the outdoor competitive season. Cross-country running is continued once or twice per week. Weight training is used Monday and Wednesday, with emphasis on maintaining the strength which has been gained in the two previous phases of preparation. One hundred twenty-yard hurdle work on the grass is done twice a week. The remainder of the practice time is spent reviewing jumping technique. Stop action movies are a must during this period.

In preparing for a meet, a measuring tape should be available to mark the one or two check marks that will be used in competition. In getting steps, consider wind direction and the type of running surface. With the wind at the athlete's back or on a very fast runway, the mark indicating the start of the run will have to be moved a number of inches farther away from the take-off board.

July through August

During these summer months, general conditioning should be maintained by participating three to four days a week in some type of relaxing, physical activity. The amount and degree of physical activity during this fourth phase will depend upon the mental and physical condition of the athlete on completion of the competitive outdoor season.

Clarence Robinson, as a senior at Washington High School in East Chicago, Indiana, long jumped 22 feet, 9 inches and did not triple jump until his freshman year in college.

1963 Freshman Year: Long jump 24 feet, 7½ inches; triple jump 47 feet, 2¾ inches.

1964 Sophomore Year: Long jump 25 feet, 5½ inches; triple jump 50 feet, 4½ inches.

1965 Junior Year: Long jump 26 feet, 9¼ inches (third best in the history of the long jump). Triple jump 52 feet, 8¼ inches (National Collegiate record). 1965 Drake Relays long jump-triple jump champion. 1965 Kansas Relays long jump-triple jump champion and outstanding athlete of the meet. 1965 Western Athletic Conference long jump-triple jump champion. 1965 NCAA gold medal winner in the long jump and triple jump. Robinson was the first man to win this double since 1931.

This 6 foot, 1½ inch athlete, weighing 165 pounds, is a senior at the University of New Mexico, majoring in education. He is a quiet, soft-spoken, polite person, nicknamed "Clank" by his teammates. Robinson has developed from a rather frail, quick speed boy into a mature, physically strong athlete, yet still retains great spring and speed. Clarence runs cross-country two to three times per week six months of the year and does weight training work nine months of the year. He has unlimited potential in both the long jump and the triple jump. Robinson has improved an average of one foot each year in the long jump and approximately two and one-half feet each year in the triple jump. We believe he will be the greatest long jumper and triple jumper of all time.

Clarence hits the take-off board with his left foot in both the long jump and triple jump and uses the same length run in both, 126 feet. His splits in collegiate record triple jump were 19 feet, 2 inches; 15 feet, 10 inches; and 17 feet, 8¼ inches.

After he has warmed up properly, the athlete should run through the step a few times at regular runway speed. If he runs slower than normal, he will usually overstride, miss his take-off board, and lose confidence in his check marks at a very inopportune time. On the first jump in competition, the athlete will probably still not be completely warmed up. Therefore, the run will lengthen a few inches on the second and third jumps and these jumps often are the best jumps in competition. Of course, in meets with good competition, the experienced athlete will often get off his best jump on the last jump. The length of the spike used on the runway is important. Spikes need only be long enough to maintain traction. When they are too long, they dig into the runway, cause loss of speed, loss of balance, and can produce a muscle pull. Many jumpers hit a runway with forty steps, each step driving four to six nails one-half inch in to the surface, and then at take-off, drive those same four to six nails one-half inch into a board.

It is impossible for an athlete who is doubling to take every trial in the triple jump in each meet for the entire competitive season. We believe a maximum of two or three long jumps and two or three triple jumps in each meet are the most one athlete should do, if he wishes to double in top condition, mental and physical, throughout the track season.

22

TRIPLE JUMP TRAINING

Dean Hayes
Middle Tennessee State University

What is the triple jump? How is it approached in training? Is it a three-phase event?

The triple jump is an event in which the United States has generally taken second place to eastern Europeans, an event in which a limited number of Americans have really been successful. Yet, America does have great athletes who should be capable of bounding great lengths. The United States has great long jumpers, why not equally great triple jumpers?

Barry McClure came to Middle Tennessee State University in the fall of 1969. He was the Georgia state champion in a small high school, Carrollton, Georgia, and was coached by Vernon Wilkes. His longest jump in high school was 47 feet, ½ inch but he did record a 48 foot, 6 inch jump at the Atlanta Track Classic in a summer meet. Barry was long-legged, slim of build, and about 5 feet, 10 inches tall.

In analyzing Barry, we decided that he must learn to have *thinking feet,* increase his strength, and learn to run with balance and relaxation. We felt we should work on a few things, but emphasize doing them well.

The material in this article covers the *on the field phase* of our training program. Emphasis must be placed on weight training as another important phase of the workouts and a great deal of time and effort should be spent on this work.

The triple jump: Illustrations 1-6.

The triple jump: Illustrations 7-16.

For thinking feet, two drills called benches (Diagrams 1 and 2) were used. These benches, 12 inches wide and 20 inches high, were placed on the runway in a line. The approach should be relaxed but quick and the double arm motion should be used in these drills.

To increase strength, the jumpers did hops, steps, and pop-ups. In this segment, the main emphasis was to achieve good reach and knee lift movement. The procedure used is as follows: Hops -R-R-R-R-R- etc. or -L-L-L-L- etc. Do some of these on each leg. Steps -R-L-R-L-R- etc. Pop-ups—Short approach, pop-up as used by the long jumpers.

We believe in hurdling to learn balance. It also teaches an aggressive approach. We start with low hurdles and work up as high as the jumper can hurdle. The hurdles are spaced 10 yards apart.

To develop relaxation, the jumpers did regular sprint work: 25 yards—35 yards—50 yards. Some days they ran 100's, 220's or 300's.

Basically, our sequence of workouts would be: *Monday.* Hops, steps, and pop-ups. Running. Lift weights. *Tuesday.* Benches. Hurdles. Running. *Wednesday.* Hops, steps, and pop-ups. Running. Lift weights. *Thursday.* Benches. Hurdles. Running. *Friday.* Hops, steps, and pop-ups. Running. Lift weights.

This work requires concentration and effort. It is relatively simple and doing it correctly is important.

Triple jumping is an unnatural movement and repetition of the basic movements is important. Our jumpers do very little, if any, jumping other than in meets. However, short approach jumping is recommended for beginners.

These workouts are the basic on the field work of all our triple jumpers. Barry McClure is the only jumper who came to Middle Tennessee as a triple jumper, yet we have had others jump over 50 feet. Tommy Haynes has probably contributed a great deal to Barry's success because they do their workouts together and work well together. Good effort must be put forth every day, especially when it is considered that a jumper's greatest rival among collegiate jumpers is his own teammate. Tommy Haynes triple jumped 49 feet, 5 inches on the first jump he ever took in his life. He placed in the NCAA indoor in 1973 with 51 feet, 11 ¾ inches and has just barely scratched 52 feet, 11 ¾ inches.

Triple jumping is an event that requires skill, strength, and work just like any other event in track and field. Meet directors must be encouraged to include the triple jump and states must work for the development of this event. Coaches would then have another event in which more athletes could find success and a chance for recognition. Perhaps coaches have or can develop another Barry McClure.

During our nine years at Middle Tennessee State University we have had three triple jumpers over 50 feet.

Barry McClure was the NCAA indoor triple jump champion in 1972 and 1973. He set a new collegiate indoor record of 54 feet, 1¾ inches and has a lifetime best of 54 feet, 4¼ inches. He has scored more points in NCAA meets than any other triple jumper and was recognized as an All-American in seven of the eight NCAA championships in which he competed.

Tommy Haynes (25 feet, 11 inches and 51 feet, 11¾ inches) has been a NCAA finalist in the long jump or triple jump four times, and Terry Scott (24 feet, ½ inch and 50 feet, ¼ inch) has been a NCAA finalist in the triple jump once.

23
IMPROVING YOUR TRIPLE JUMP

Douglas P. Mack
Mesa Community College

In this article, we will discuss suggested points which will help in the competitive evaluation of the triple jump. The relationship of the three parts of the jump will be covered, and the phases of the run will be broken down into the hop phase, step phase, and the jump. No one part of the total jump should be emphasized to the point where the other segments are appreciably affected. It is important that, as the jumper completes one part of the jump, he is in position for the next part of the total effort. The height of the hop and the step must be minimized to maintain horizontal speed for the jump phase. The more height there is at the take-off, the less horizontal speed will be maintained upon landing. Take-off angles for the three parts of the jump are shown in Diagram 1.

The Run

Diagram 1

When discussing the run, speed is of great importance, but so is position at the take-off board. A jumper should approach the board with controlled speed. The crouch is not emphasized as it is in the long jump. Height from the board is not desirable. A *gather* at the board is not important, because the hips should remain forward and not level as they do in the long jump.

While the jumper is in the hop phase, the take-off is forward of the board, and speed is the important factor at this point. He should think of the take-off as being from the ball of his foot, (actually it is not), and his weight should be forward. A low angle of flight off the board is important in maintaining horizontal speed. The jumper's opposite knee should glide forward —not be driven up. His center of gravity should be only slightly behind his take-off foot as it makes contact with the board. His arms should work alternately as they do in sprinting.

In the flight the jumper's opposite leg, not the take-off leg, should drop back behind the vertical plane of the take-off leg, as far as possible, without causing the upper body to lean forward. It will be brought through again during the step phase of the triple jump. The take-off leg should flex slightly for balance and in preparation for landing at the conclusion of the hop. His head and chest should be up, eyes straight ahead, back straight, and weight slightly forward. Both arms should be dropping back behind the vertical plane of his body (Diagram 2).

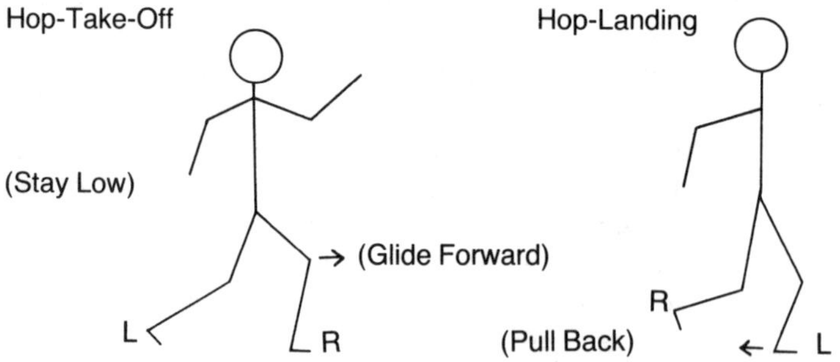

Hop-Take-Off

(Stay Low)

→ (Glide Forward)

L   R   (Pull Back)   L

R

Diagram 2

Hop-Landing

In the step phase, the take-off leg should be in the same position it is in the hop. The take-off foot should touch flat with the foot moving backward, leg pulling, before the foot makes contact with the runway. This creates the same effect as a child keeping a scooter moving forward. As the take-off foot makes contact with the runway, the knee of the opposite leg should drive forward and up to a position even with the horizontal plane of the jumper's hip. The jumper's foot should be in a flexed position, toes up, and directly below the knee. His knee should be brought through high for position and not for added lift, because horizontal speed is still the primary factor, not vertical height. The arms should be brought forward and upward for balance and added forward momentum. He should keep his head and chest high, and his weight slightly forward.

When in flight, the jumper's take-off leg should flex slightly and remain back behind his hips. The opposite leg should remain in knee high position, delayed at hip level, until just before landing. This adds considerably to the length of the step. Again, the foot should be flexed and under the knee. The arms begin dropping back behind the vertical plane of the body (Diagram 3).

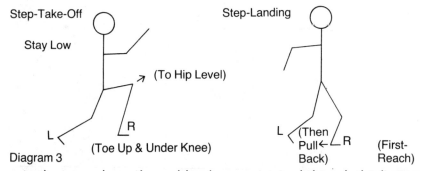

Diagram 3

In the jump phase, if speed has been maintained through the first two phases, the hop and the step, then the horizontal speed should be sufficient for the concluding phase, the jump. The take-off angle, height, should be greater for the jump, because horizontal speed is not important at the conclusion of this phase, the final landing. Some steps in obtaining the lift are as follows: Increase the take-off angle with the take-off leg. The knee of the opposite leg should be driven through high. The jumper's arms should be driven upward. His head and chest should be held high. Also, in coming off the step, the take-off foot for the jump should reach slightly. This reach levels the hips, which is important for greater take-off angle. The reach will decrease the amount of speed for the jump phase, unless a modification is made. This modification is in the take-off leg moving backward even before the foot comes in contact with the runway. The leg should be pulling, using the same principle as the take-off for the step phase. In order to retain forward speed, it is important for the body weight to slide forward before leg extension begins.

In the flight, if the jumper has good position and speed going into the jump phase, then the step and a half method should be used. If the speed at the point of the jump is not adequate and lack of time during the flight is a factor, the jumper should use any method available to get his legs extended and his heels high in front of his body. The more speed there is at the take-off, the higher the jumper's heels can be and still be effective. When adequate speed is present, the hips are level at take-off and the heels are high. If speed is inadequate the hips should be forward to salvage momentum. Thus, the jumper's heels cannot be as high as desired.

In landing, the jumper's feet should land about ten inches apart.

In landing, the jumper's feet should land about ten inches apart. As the feet break the sand, the knees should bend and the body weight should pass forward through the knees. The jumper's arms should be driven backward timed with the bending of his knees. His chin should be on his chest as soon as his heels touch the sand (Diagram 4).

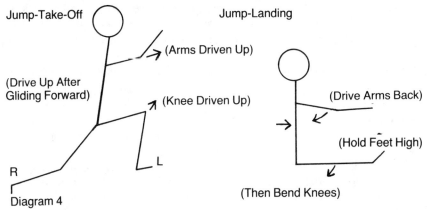

Jump-Take-Off

Jump-Landing

(Arms Driven Up)

(Drive Up After Gliding Forward)

(Knee Driven Up)

(Drive Arms Back)

(Hold Feet High)

L

R

(Then Bend Knees)

Diagram 4

A mistake is too much height off the board, hop take-off, because forward speed is decreased for the last two step and jump phases of the total jump. A correction would be to shorten the last step so the body weight is over the take-off leg—weight forward. The jumper should think of taking off from the ball of his foot. He should check to see whether his opposite knee is coming through too high. If it is, let the knee glide forward. Possibly the step is too far back; if so, move it closer to the board.

Another mistake could be too much height during the step. In correcting this error, (which happens because the knee of the opposite leg is brought through forcibly) the jumper might emphasize height on the take-off for the step. He should practice the delayed step drill with emphasis on driving the opposite knee high and riding it out while driving forward with the take-off leg. This will cause the jumper to learn the rhythm of this difficult part of the jump.

Another mistake could be that the body weight gets too far forward during any part of the triple jump. Remember, the body should be in a semisitting position at all times. Keep the head and chest up and the eyes straight ahead.

Failure to get the knee of the opposite leg high during the step could be another mistake. This problem involves bringing the knee through low, which makes it more difficult to keep the body in an erect position during the step. Also, the low knee decreases the distance of the step. The triple jumper should learn and practice the delayed step drill and the hop, step drill. These drills will teach the jumper proper position and body lean.

The last type of error concerns the jumper who has difficulties with injuries to his knees and ankles. Before any drills or jumping, the athlete should participate in a weight-training program with emphasis on leg conditioning. All drills and jumping should take place on a grass area. Since a jumper's legs take a great deal of pounding, a soft surface is desirable. When the ankles and/or knees start to hurt, stay off hard runway surfaces. The coach should check to see that the jumper's foot is moving backward as he lands coming off the hop and the step. If the foot is moving, floating forward, there will be a tremendous jar upon landing. This would also decrease the amount of forward speed.

A weight training program should precede all activities pertaining to the triple jump. Triple jumpers should have strong and durable joints and legs to prevent injuries that might occur during strenuous drills and/or jumping. Following is a sample workout:

Circuit Drill (upper body)—We have five exercises which our jumpers use. These consist of one set of ten repetitions for each exercise, with no rest period between exercises: reverse curls, military press, vertical rowing, regular curls, and an include or bench press. All of these exercises are performed without putting down the weight, and the same weight is used for all exercises.

The abdominal exercises we use are jackknives—(two sets of 25 repetitions) and leg raises from a bar (two sets of 10 repetitions).

We perform six leg exercises: leg squats (two sets of 10 repetitions), leg press (two sets of 10 repetitions), squat jumps (two sets of 10 repetitions), squat lunges (two sets of 10 repetitions), leg curls (three sets of 15 repetitions) and leg pull through (two sets of 15 repetitions).

JUMPING DRILLS

There are two purposes in using the drill system: To improve the timing and rhythm of the jumper and to strengthen the jumper in all phases of triple jumping. The following drills are recommended:

Hop-Step Drill. Run at half speed, go through the hop-step phase of the total jump. Then run at half speed and repeat. Emphasis should be on body position, arm lift, and take-off trajectory.

Delayed Step Drill. This drill is similar to a running stride, with the following adjustments: At the point of the knee lift, the jumper should delay until his foot is ready to land. His foot should be flexed and directly under his knee. The take-off foot should remain in contact with the ground longer than it would in a normal running stride. The arms should work simultaneously, not alternately as in running. They should lift forward and upward in time with the knee lift. Concentrate on jumping forward, not puward.

Hop Drill. Hop, using the same leg, with emphasis on forward movement.

It is recommended that 30 yards be used in the beginning, building up to 60 yards, and eventually to 90 yards. The jumpers should perform each drill twice before going to the next drill. Weight jackets and ankle weights can be used after basic rhythm patterns have been established.

Endurance Running. The early weight training program should be complemented with 330's and 220's. The ligaments and tendons of the jumper's hip and leg regions must be strengthened properly to decrease the chance of injuries later in the year. This stength running should continue all year, but speed interval work should be added during the second half of the training season. An example of speed interval training would be as follows: 110×12 (grass). 110's accelerations (accelerate and float at 3-points during the 110). Repeat 50-yard dashes (blocks).

Step Work. The run and approach to the board are important. While the amount of speed is important, the consistency of the run and approach is the essential thing. The jumper has many things to think about during the approach and it is important that the step is not one of them. There are many variables which contribute to the inconsistency of the step. These are: Wind (with the jumper—against the jumper). Different runway surfaces. Inexperience (includes the lack of preparation). Unevenness of stride. Competitive pressure.

The jumper should check his step at least three times a week. It is recommended that he do the hop part of the total jump to check the mark when he is actually planning to jump. It will be different from just running through.

Low hurdle work is recommended if the jumper is having trouble with evenness of stride. It is best to use two step markers. These will give the jumper a safety valve check point after he starts down the runway. This second check point should not be located any closer to the take-off board than 60 feet. From this point on the jumper should concentrate on position at the take-off board.

In order to be successful, the triple jumper should have speed, strength, position, technique, consistency, and good attitude.

24

PREPARATION OF A TRIPLE JUMPER

Jake Pagano
North Tonawanda, New York, High School

In order to decide what physical conditioning is required for the triple jump, it is necessary to break down the fitness factor into four areas of concern:

- General background of fitness.
- Running speed.
- Leg and back strength.
- Leg power and flexibility.

GENERAL BACKGROUND OF FITNESS

The need for this type of work will vary from athlete to athlete. In the case of the young athlete, whose background of general conditioning is probably small, there is always a need for a fair period of general conditioning. This period should consist of cross-country running, interval running, general calisthenics, and basic weight training. It provides the core of fitness on which the more intense and specific training can be based. The purpose of a general calisthenics program is to improve metabolism, circulation, relaxation, and general muscular development. Cross-country and interval running develop endurance or the ability to withstand fatigue and the stresses set up by prolonged activity. It improves the cardiovascular system, preparing the individual for harder training which will be necessary at a later stage or phase in the training period.

It is impossible to give a training schedule that is entirely suitable for everyone, but the following is a sample program of general conditioning.

FIRST WEEK

Jog 880 yards.

General calisthenics—jumping jacks, push-ups, sit-ups, hurdler's stretch, windmills, and toe touches. Any additional exercises that the coach feels are needed may be included.

Basic weight training—Monday, Wednesday, and Friday—military press, two arm curl, dead lift, toe raise, bench press, side bender, half squats, and leg press.

Jog 2 miles.

SECOND WEEK

Jog 880 yards. General calisthenics—same as the first week, but increase the number of repetitions. Basic weight training—same exercises, but increase weight. Jog 2½ miles.

THIRD WEEK

Jog 880 yards. General calisthenics. Basic weight training. Jog 3 miles.

FOURTH WEEK

Jog 880 yards. General calisthenics. Basic weight training. Four × 330's one-half lap walk between each. Jog 880 yards.

FIFTH WEEK

Jog 880 yards. General calisthenics. Basic weight training. Six × 330's one-half lap walk between each. Jog 880 yards.

RUNNING SPEED

Basically, the triple jump is a speed event and every effort must be made to improve the jumper's approach speed. Often a jumper's technique improves without similar changes taking place in approach speed. Therefore, as a rule, the gains made in distance are small. A jumper's ability to run fast over 30 to 40 yards is more important than his ability to run a fast 100 yards. Thus training should be directed toward improving his ability to run fast 30-to 40-yard dashes with the ultimate aim being to improve his ability to attack the takeoff board at speeds as close as possible to his maximum.

Sprinting speed is determined by a number of alterable factors including the strength of the muscles involved in the running action, flexibility, explosive power, reaction time, stride, and form or technique. Efficient sprinting form wil not be developed without continuous practice in these areas.

In order to develop efficient sprinting speed, athletes must be constantly aware of body lean, leg, knee, arm, and hip action. They must be working continuously toward improvement of these factors. Correct form constitutes a means of attaining maximum results without undue lost motion or wasted energy. Numerous researchers have identified the essentials of efficient sprinting as follows:

- Use of a forceful push off the rear leg.
- High knee lift.
- Placement of the foot directly beneath the center of gravity.

The rewards of good form or ideal technique are increased movement efficiency, limited energy expenditure, optimum use of the components of strength, explosive power, and flexibility, and ultimately increased sprinting speed, resulting in longer jumps.

LEG AND BACK STRENGTH

This is the gradual build-up of strength through the use of weight training and hopping exercises to improve the ability to absorb landing shocks at the end of the hop and step, independent of technique.

WEIGHT TRAINING

Without knowing the specific needs of an individual athlete, it is impossible to prescribe a weight training schedule listing all the starting poundages for every lift. It is necessary for the coach to work with the athlete and discover his particular needs from practical experience.

Jumpers must plan to build up strength throughout the year. They need great leg power in relation to their body weight, because weight determines their relative strength in jumping.

The following exercises develop the muscle groups that are needed most for jumping. Heel raise (from a board). Donkey heel raise. Half squats. Quarter squat (very heavy weight). Full squat (light weight). Leg press. Straddle lift (straight back). Stiff-legged dead lift. Leg curl. Leg extension. Step-ups. Bounding split squats. Almost all of these exercises can be found in any weight training book, with the exception of the hip flexor (Diagram 1).

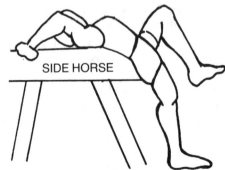

SIDE HORSE

Diagram 1

Another important method of developing leg and back strength is the use of hopping exercises such as hopping down steps, hopping up steps, jumps with weights on the back, and hopping on and off boxes. These exercises should be done along with the weight training program.

LEG POWER AND FLEXIBILITY

This is perhaps the key to success in the triple jump. Explosive power is essential for a triple jumper if he is to obtain his best jumps. One of the best methods of developing explosive reactive-ballistic contractions in muscles is called plyometric, and it has been used overseas for specific power development.

The exercises are based on the principle of pre-stretching the muscles in a gathering phase to use the kinetic energy developed in this phase in the following contraction. In other words, the athlete is developing the possibility of a higher muscle contraction by using kinetic energy from breaking a motion opposite the intended action. In developing plyometric exercises, the breaking or gathering phase should be as short as possible and performed without changing the basic pattern of the movement. This allows for maximum strength to be developed in the second part of the acceleration phase. Each repetition should be performed flat out to develop a maximum effort.

In most plyometric exercises the athlete takes off from an elevated position with one leg slightly forward to develop a vertical position for the fall. The landing takes place on the ball of the foot with the knees bent to an angle which allows sufficient gathering and a smooth change to the upward drive.

Exercises can be performed landing and taking off from one or both legs. Generally, it is better to progress by increasing the elevation instead of using additional resistance of weights and weight jackets.

Following are a few examples of plyometric exercises.

Exercise 1 is a rebound jump with a double-legged takeoff after the fall. The athlete reaches as high as possible. The same exercise can be used from a higher elevation, but the rebound takeoff is performed from one leg only.

Exercise 2 is a jump from elevation with the rebound performed in the long jump fashion.

Exercise 3 is a jump from elevation, landing for the rebound into a high triple jump step, followed by a jump for distance.

The coach can develop many exercises of this type that will be a great help to the athlete.

Flexibility is important for any athletic event, but being able to extend the muscles through a full range of motion is vital in producing maximum performance. Following is a list of flexibility exercises that are excellent. They should be done as slowly as possible. Do each exercise 2 or 3 times slowly.

Diagram 2

Exercise 1 (Diagram 2). Lie flat on the back, flex the knees, and slowly draw the right knee up as close to the chest as possible. Slowly straighten the leg, let it fall to the floor limp and relaxed. Pull it up again to the flexed starting position. Now do the same thing with the other leg. Repeat the exercise, using alternate legs.

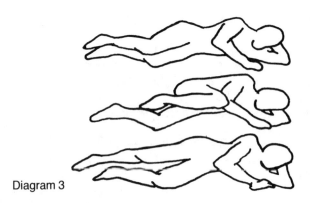

Diagram 3

Exercise 2 (Diagram 3). Lie on the left side with the head and neck in a relaxed position. Keep both knees flexed and the hips slightly flexed. Slide the right knee as close to the head as is comfortably possible, and then slowly extend the leg until it is completely straight. Let the leg drop to the floor relaxed. Do the exercise two or three time, and then turn to the right side and do the exercise with the left leg.

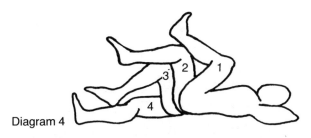

Diagram 4

Exercise 3 (Diagram 4). Lie on the back with both knees flexed. Pull both knees up to the chest. Then lower the legs gradually, straightening them at the same time, until they finally reach the floor.

Diagram 5

Exercise 4 (Diagram 5). Lie on the back with the knees flexed. Raise both the head and the right knee and try to make them meet. Do not try too hard. At first, the athlete will probably not succeed, but eventually he will. Return to the starting position and do the same exercise with the head and left knee.

Diagram 6

Exercise 5 (Diagram 6). Assume a kneeling position, resting on the hands and knees. Arch the back similar to a cat, and drop the head at the same time. Then reverse the arch by bringing up the head and forming a U with the spine.

Diagram 7

Exercise 6 (Diagram 7). Lie on the back, both knees flexed, arms at sides. Bring one knee up as close as possible to the face, raise that leg straight up in the air, and lower it slowly to the floor. The athlete should feel a pull in his hamstring as he does this. Return to the starting position. Relax for a moment before doing the same exercise with the other knee.

Exercise 7. Turn over on the stomach. Let the head rest comfortably on the folded hands. Then tighten the seat muscles. Hold that position for two seconds, and then relax.

Following is a list of foot and ankle exercises which we feel are very important due to the tremendous amount of stress that is placed on the foot and ankle during jumping.

• Remove the shoes and stand on the floor with the feet together. Extend the arms forward, shoulder width apart, and place the palms of the hands on the back of a chair. Then rise on the toes as high as possible. Repeat 25 times (Diagram 8).

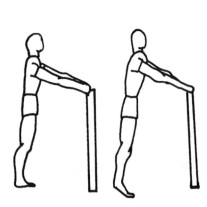

Diagram 8   Diagram 9

• Use the same starting position described for the previous exercise. Roll the feet outward so that the weight of the body is supported on the outer edges of the feet. Return to the starting position. Repeat 25 times (Diagram 9).

Diagram 10

- Roll the feet outward so that the weight of the body is supported on the outer edges of the feet (Diagram 10). Roll forward up on the toes as high as possible. Lower the heels and return to the starting position. Repeat 15 times.

Diagram 11

- Kneel on the floor, feet together, body upright, and toes pointing backward (Diagram 11). Lean back and place the finger tips on the floor. Place the palms of the hands on the floor if possible. Return to the starting position. Repeat 15 times.

Diagram 12

- Lean back and place the finger tips on the floor without changing the position of the body. Place the hands on the hips (Diagram 12). Return to the starting position. Repeat 10 times.

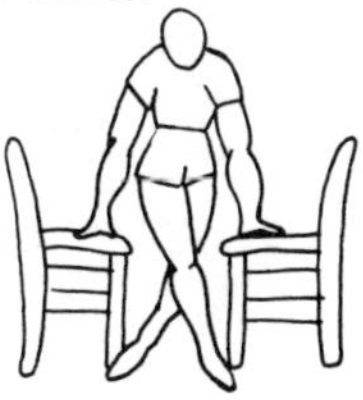

Diagram 13

- Sit on the floor. Bend both knees and cross the right leg over the left far enough to set the outer edges of both feet flat on the floor. Place a chair on either side close enough to place the palms of the hands on the seats of the chairs (Diagram 13). With the aid of the hands if necessary, straighten the knees to a standing position. Do not move the position of the feet. Return to the starting position. Repeat 15 times.

Part 3
The
Vertical
Jumps

25
THE CONVENTIONAL STRADDLE JUMP

Roy Griak
University of Minnesota

These excellent pictures of Tom Stuart clearing 6 feet, 9 inches in the high jump at the 1968 Drake Relays show the technique of the conventional straddle jump.

Illustration 1. The angle of approach at 38°, with four walking, and seven running steps shows Stuart's approach. We like to have the approach be as relaxed as possible so that the jumper can reach the crossbar without tension. This is an accelerated run, carefully measured, and the approach speed must be controlled tempo at take-off. Special emphasis is placed on a double arm action, with the arms back when the right foot is in contact with the approach area. The settle action of the hip begins during the last two strides.

Illustrations 2 and 3. Tom's last stride is low and flat with heel-to-toe action of the left plant foot. His jumping foot is kept in the line of direction of approach. At this point it will be noticed that Stuart's upper body mass is in back of his center of gravity, which is essential to get proper body lift at take-off. The body mass passes over the braced left take-off foot. Both arms and the lead leg start forward in a coordinated action. This type of action of the lower center mass, lay back action, and initial action of the bent lead leg will enable Tom to exert as much force as possible downward against the ground. He can apply more force for longer period of time and get the vertical lift from his body strength.

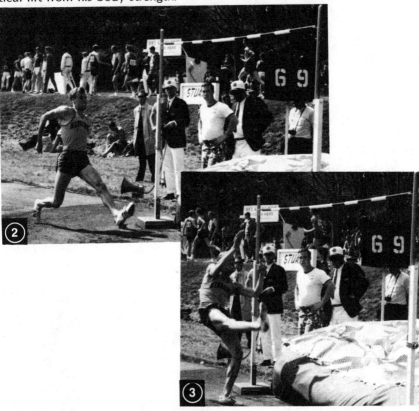

Illustration 3. Stuart's arm and legs come at the same time. Notice the straight lead leg in the illustration. Illustration 2 shows a bent lead leg. He starts with a bent lead leg, and shortens the lever in order to get greater speed with his lead leg. Illustration 3 shows a straight lead leg, thus a longer lever and greater force applied to lifting action for a longer period of time. Tom is leaning towards the crossbar with his inside shoulder. This action, which we frown on, will affect his vertical lift.

Illustrations 4 and 5. The timing of the lead leg and double arm action as the body mass passes over is clearly shown in this illustration. Stuart comes off the toes of his jumping foot, with the high point of the lead leg placed above the crossbar. Timing must be perfect to exert the greatest amount of force on the ground.

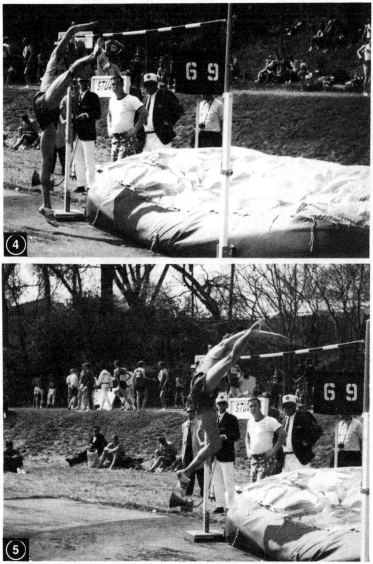

Illustration 5. Stuart is leading over the crossbar in clockwise hinge action with his lead leg, outside arm, and head going over first.

Illustration 6. Tom's spin-roll layout on the crossbar is determined by the technique at take-off. His lead leg is placed above the crossbar, right arm action is down, and his back is towards the right standard. The action of the right arm will quicken the spin-roll and clear the left side of the body over the crossbar. Stuart's left arm is in poor position for bar clearance. We would rather have the left arm tucked in close to the body and not in chicken-wing fashion as is shown. We strive for a passive left side, and depend on the action of the right arm for the spin-roll over the crossbar.

Illustration 7. Notice the good action of Stuart's right arm. His left arm which shows improper technique could cause a delayed action of spin-roll. We would like to see a wider spread of the thighs for bar clearance.

Illustrations 8 and 9. The bar is cleared by maintaining a wide spread of the thighs as the spin-roll begins. The toe should be kept in an upward position to complete the roll over the crossbar.

Illustrations 9 and 10. The trailing leg should remain in a bent position, with the toe pointed upward. Faulty left arm technique is clearly visible in Illustration 9. We feel this action has delayed the action of straight leg clearance.

Illustration 10. As shown, Stuart's body landing in the center of the pit would indicate that he had good transfer of horizontal speed approach, to vertical lift at the take-off.

26

THE FLOP HIGH JUMP *

Don Chu
Cal State University Hayward
and
Sue Humphrey
Arizona State University

INTRODUCTION

Since Dick Fosbury "backed" into a gold medal at the 1968 Olympics, high jumpers on every level, male and female, have taken up his unique back-to-the-bar flop style.

With so many athletes working on a revolutionary style, changes are inevitable. And so it has been with the flop. Some of the refinements stem from biomechanical analysis, others from individual adaptations.

The question continually asked of coaches is: "Is there a right way to do the flop?" It is these authors' opinion that there is, but that allowances can be made for individual variations so long as the jumper knows what he/she is doing.

FLOP HIGH JUMP TECHNIQUE

Coaches, athletes, and especially spectators marvel at the consistency of top caliber high jumpers. Outstanding heights are reached meet after meet, competition after competition.

*Reprinted from the book, **The Athletics Congress' Track and Field Coaching Manual.** Used by permission of the author and the publisher.

The key to success in high jumping is consistency.

The definition of "consistency" includes a statement on the ability of the high jumper to engage in precise repetition of physical movement. Great jumpers do not "warm up" to great heights. They are, in fact, ready to perform maximal jumps from attempt number one until they finally fail on three attempts. In order to accomplish this, the high jumper must fully understand the meaning and importance of the approach to the bar.

The purpose of the approach is more than simply running to the bar and taking off. The approach is intended to place the jumper in the best position for take-off. This position is not a static point of balance as captured on film. It is a dynamic position representing not only balance, but speed of limb movement and the summation of physical forces.

Approach Shape: By the very shape of the approach in high jumping, certain mechanical advantages are gained which will aid the high jumper in attaining his potential height. The most often used approach in flopping is that of a "J" shape. Since it is begun in a straight line, it allows for the development of speed, built up, and then transferred to the slight curve at the end (usually three to five steps in length). Running through a quarter of a circle allows the jumper to build "centripetal" force (the opposite, or release from this force is better known as "centrifugal") prior to take-off. It is this force which will throw the high jumper over the bar after he/she breaks contact with the ground at take-off.

The approach length is generally nine to eleven strides. Longer approaches tend to create too many variables for consistency and fewer strides do not allow the high jumper to develop enough speed for maximal forces to be applied to the ground. It is important to understand the following relationship: the speed of running an approach is the maximal speed which can be controlled. This will be further clarified in this chapter. Since the take-off spot is at the standard nearest the jumper the question of approach radius often arises. This distance will vary with the height and limb length of the jumper. Data from USOC Olympic Development camps tend to indicate that an arc radius of 18 feet is very comfortable and effective. This might range from 15 to 20 feet depending again on how tall the jumper is, and how effectively he/she can run the arc. If there are three to five steps within the arc itself, that leaves four to eight strides straight on. It is recommended that jumpers take a ten-step approach with a five-step lead-in and five-step curve.

First Step: The first step is the most underrated and overlooked portion of the approach. It sets the tempo of the whole approach because it is a result of how much force the jumper uses to initiate his/her approach run. If this step varies, it means the jumper is using a different amount of force to push off each time. This, in turn, means different stride length, speed and take-off point. To technicians, however, this step requires essence of consistency. It should be measured, marked and practiced.

Steps Two-Five: These steps are in a straight line. After pushing off, they reflect the tempo or pace established by the first step. The body position of the jumper should be balanced. His/her body should be over the foot when it contacts the ground. The jumper must not be leaning forward in an attempt to accelerate since this would place his/her hips in an ineffective position for take-off. Likewise, a position of leaning back while running will also result in an ineffective position, mechanically speaking, for take-off. Thus, the run is a "controlled" maximal-speed approach.

The Curve: A "turn mark" should always be placed on the approach surface during practice. This mark enables the jumper to develop a kinesthetic awareness of when to change the approach and start to "lean-in" on the curve and build his/her centripetal force. The lean position is vital. It is important to remember this will be what projects the jumper over the bar at take-off. If the jumper fails to lean-in, then he/she must actually apply an eccentric or off-center thrust at take-off, that will only detract from his/her potential height. Film studies show this angle to be approximately 10-15° of body lean to the inside of the curve.

The Last Three Steps: The final strides going into take-off must now change. A slight acceleration going into the take-off mark is desirable. This is not to be mistaken with "changing gears". There is no hard, discernable change in approach speed. In actual viewing, it appears as a "smooth" and "quick" approach to take-off. Acceleration at the end of the approach allows the jumper to actually shorten the stride length slightly and "catch" the body's center of gravity on the rise. This is the most important aspect of the approach for any of the jumping events.

THE PLANT

The outside foot should be planted almost parallel to the bar pointing to the opposite standard. This will allow the inside knee to drive across the body to the opposite hip, in order to rotate it. Since rotation must begin with the plant foot on the ground, any improper placement of this foot will disrupt the jumper's ability to achieve the back-to-the-bar position.

The more the foot points toward the bar, the most difficult it will become to achieve rotation. In fact, the jumper can injure the ankle or knee in

The penultimate stride with arm back.

attempting to rotate over a foot that is almost perpendicular to the bar. Complaints of tenderness over the outside of the ankle or the inside of the knee after jumping may stem from an improper plant.

The body, due to the acceleration and position of balance in the run, should have its center of gravity 15-18 inches behind the plant foot. The 10° body lean should have been held to this point.

The plant should be a heel-to-toe action. The rock-up may not be as pronounced as it is in the straddle, but it is still essential.

Because of his/her acceleration during the approach, the jumper may require a stronger braking action with the rear spike in order to check the linear motion. But he/she must still try to run off the end of the approach and transfer linear speed into vertical velocity. This action is easier to achieve with the flop than with the straddle.

The jumper must avoid planting on the front part of the foot. That sort of plant would prevent the checking of linear speed and the development of vertical power with the ankle and foot. These members and the muscles around them must be fully extended to develop the maximal power from them. Planting on the forefoot will likely cause the athlete to drive into the bar as if he/she were long-jumping.

ARM ACTION

The arm action should resemble the sprinter's, but not with the same rigid pumping action. The arms should be relaxed with the elbow bent enough to allow the thumb area to pass at hip joint level. On the second to last (penultimate) stride, the arms should gather and synchronize with what will be the lead leg.

For the athlete who takes off on the left foot, the sequence of foot strikes through the penultimate and last strides is left-right-left. Since the normal arm action in running is reciprocal, the right arm will be forward when the left foot strikes the ground.

The athlete must be taught to let the right arm remain forward as he/she moves to the right foot, and then bring the left arm together with the right. At this juncture, both arms are synchronized with the right or lead leg.

As the athlete moves through the last stride to the plant, both arms remain synchronized with the right leg so that they will be back on the body as the jumper makes the plant.

As the jumper begins the lead leg drive, both arms move forward at the same time. Considerable thrust can be developed with a double arm action. The arms should begin to bend as the athlete swings them through so that they remain in tight with the right knee. That is, as they swing through, they remain flexed until the force of the arm swing is directly vertical and in the same place as the knee drive.

The take-off.

THE TAKE-OFF

The take-off is a continuation of the plant. As the foot rocks to the toe, the drive leg begins to pass the take-off leg, with the knee driving upward.

Two points are essential in good leg action:

First, the ankle of the take-off leg must fully extend or plantar-flex. Anything less than a full ankle extension as take-off will result in a loss of power.

Second, the lead knee must be driven away from the bar (for rotation) to the opposite standard and rise to at least waist height for full power development. The lower part of the lead leg must be perpendicular to the ground at this point. Any action which carries the lower leg out away from the vertical will cause the jumper to carry along the bar and fail to achieve enough height or rotation to clear it.

Coaching hint: Tell the athlete to keep everything "tight" and to drive the knee up, across the body, and away from the bar toward the opposite standard. The turning action of getting the back to the bar must originate on the ground.

By keeping everything in tight at take-off, the jumper will achieve a perpendicular position to the ground and develop all forces in a vertical direction, thus helping to attain maximum height.

The lead knee should continue to drive up after the take-off leg has left the ground. If the lead knee is driven properly, the legs should be spread as maximum height is attained over the bar. The athlete should attempt to drive the knee to the height of the bar. Whenever the athlete's knees are close together as they come over the bar, it indicates a lack of lead knee drive and a flight path that will not achieve full potential.

Measuring the Approach: Athletes have toyed with many ways to accurately map out their approach. The difference in facilities from week to week often plays havoc with high jumpers trying to "get their steps". The following is offered as a method of guaranteeing the measurements of an approach to be the same, regardless of where they are put down. "Triangulation" requires a single 200-foot tape. The measurements for an approach are then taken as follows:

- From the base of the standard (shaft) out to a point 'A'. This measurement should be parallel or in line with the high jump bar as it rests on the standards. Record this distance e.g., 18'.
- Run the tape out so that point B (starting point) is perpendicular to point A. Record the *total* distance on the tape e.g., actual distance from point A to B may be 50 feet, the reading on the tape measure will be standard A + B = 68 feet.
- Finally, run the tape back to point C (base of the standard shaft) and record the total distance A + B + C = Total Measurement.
- When remeasuring, lay the tape out to points A, B and C, e.g., 18, 68, 123' 6'' and the jumper will have each point of his/her approach wherever and whenever. If points A and C are firmly held, the jumper merely has to hold the tape at the measurement for point B and adjust by pulling the tape until both sides of the triangle are straight. Then by dropping the tape at this point, he/she has the starting point.

ON TOP OF THE BAR

If, once the jumper has left the ground and has driven the lead knee properly and kept this knee up, he/she will find the back to the bar in a position to be arched.

The key to arching over the bar is the position of the head and legs. If the jumper drops the head back, the body will arch and the hips will rise in an effort to clear the bar. This position is easier to obtain when the knees are spread.

The kinesiological reason for keeping the legs spread stems from the fact that the iliofemoral ligaments of the hips are tight when the thighs are close together (internally rotated). This limits the range of motion available for hip extension, which is associated with arching over the bar. Keeping the legs spread (externally rotated) allows the iliofemoral ligaments to slacken and permits more forward movement of the thigh on the hip joint and, thus, more arch.

Some coaches use verbal cues to teach their athletes to drop their head. They tell them to "look at the far corner" of the pit. This technique has its merits, but the body will tend to follow the head; and any tipping of the head to look back will tend to turn the body over on its side and cause one hip to drop. The best technique is simply to drop the head straight back and keep the legs spread.

The arms and hands may be permitted to come to a relaxed rest on or along the thighs as the athlete travels over the bar. Thus, a short powerful drive with the arms on the take—off will be followed by the arms coming to rest at the sides.

On top of the bar.

Some jumpers prefer to continue thrusting their arms up and to finally reach back with one or both. This is usually due to a lack of strength and timing in the arm drive.

The problem with this technique is that it puts the shoulder much closer to the bar early in the trajectory. Any dropping or reaching of the arms too early in the flight path will simply pull the athlete down by dropping his/her center of gravity earlier than desired.

Many athletes drill countless hours on flipping the feet up after clearing the bar with their hips. This movement is a result of the biomechanical principle known as action-reaction. Anytime the athlete wants the feet to move up, he/she need simply move the head forward from the arched position over the bar. The feet will come up and put the body in a piked position.

Some coaches teach the athlete to drop the hips as he/she feels them clear the bar. Since the path of trajectory is already determined at take-off and since the athlete usually attains an arched position over the bar, the clearance really does not have to be a dramatic effort but, rather, a subtle curling up of the head an neck. That is all that will be required to elevate the feet.

It may be noted that every jumper, when approaching maximum heights, will have very little time to bring the feet up. Hence, gross movements such as pike position, cannot be carried out efficiently at maximum heights.

It may be noted that every jumper, when approaching maximum heights, will have very little time to bring the feet up.

SUMMARY

Although the flop has many subtle variations, the jumper must still observe biomechanical laws in order to be successful:
- He/she must develop linear speed in order to exert the necessary force against the ground to achieve vertical velocity. The use of a curved approach is recommended.
- The development of vertical force is a matter of proper plant and take-off technique. The biomechanical law of transfer of momentum from a part to a whole is best served by mastering the synchronized drive-leg and double-arm lift techniques.
- The proper positioning over the bar is achieved by dropping the head back; this, coupled with the spread legs, forces the hips up. The reverse action-reaction movement forces the hips down and the feet up.

Careful utilization of this prinicple will assure the athlete of maximum height over the bar and foot clearance as the hips drop into the downward half of the flight trajectory.

An understanding of these principles and the application of them in coaching will allow the jumper to be fundamentally sound as he/she goes on to develop individual "style".

TRAINING METHODS

STRENGTH TRAINING

This is divided into five phases: first a base period devoted to quantitive work, and then later power phases for the development of maximal strength and its retention throughout the year.

Maximal Loading

This is an early pre-season period, usually July-September. During this time the jumper does a great volume of lifting, usually measured in total pounds (or kg). A larger number of sets and repetitions at moderate weight are utilized—i.e., 4-6 sets of 10-15 repetitions at 60%-70% of maximum.

Power Development Period

During this phase, emphasis is placed upon the maximal amount of weight which can be moved during a specific *time*, usually one second. This is the Russian "optimal load" concept, used to enhance faster movement response. Lifting is interspersed with jumping drills—bounding and box drills—twice a week, usually Monday and Friday. This phase generally takes place from October through January.

Example:
Half-squats
1 set × 6 reps @ 80%
optimal load (O.L.)
1 set × 8 reps @ 90%
8 single-leg hops (each leg)
1 set × 5 @ 100%
1 set × 4 @ 110%

HIGH JUMP WORK-OUTS

Three types of high-jump work-outs are used to emphasize different aspects of the training program.

Technique

This is the commonest type of session, usually done twice a week. The bar is set 6 inches below the jumper's maximum jump. 15-18 jumps are taken. Adequate rest is taken between jumps so that the jumper can be fresh and go all-out with each jump. The bar is raised 1-2 inches after the first few jumps, if all is going well. The jumper must concentrate on the specific points to be stressed in the technique during this type of session.

Endurance

This is aimed toward making many jumps during a session—up to 30 when the athlete is well-trained. Start the bar 8 inches below best jump attained. The athlete should clear 3 times at this height, and raise the bar by 2 inches. Repeat this process until the jumper misses twice—then lower the bar by one inch, which he/she should clear.

Maximal Height

The athlete takes 12-15 jumps at his/her's lifetime best and continues to jump regardless of whether the bar is cleared. Stres concentration on each jump. The athlete should try to relax and allow technique to remain and carry him/her over.

Exercise Used:

8 box jumps
1 set × 8 @ 70%

Half-squat
Inverted leg press

1 set × 10 @ 60%	Power-clean
8 in-depth jumps	Snatch
1 set × 5 @ 100%	Squat-jump

Train three times per week—M-W-F (no jump training on Wed.)

Power Transfer Period

These exercises are more specifically related to the jumping movements. They should be carried out at maximal speed. They are usually done February thru April and consist of 4 sets × 5 repetitions at maximal intensity (85-95% of single RM):

Double-legged jumps with barbell
Single legged jumps
Bounding split squats
Inverted leg press
Shoulder and biceps curl

Transition Phase-Preparation For Major Competitions

This consists of two weeks of circuit training. Set-up 6-7 stations. The athlete does 40-50% of single RM-30 seconds work, 15 seconds rest. 3 circuits.

Power Retention Phase

This helps to maintain gains made earlier, and is used during late season championship meets. One day per week. 4 sets × 6 repetitions for major muscle groups.

SEASONAL TRAINING OBJECTIVES

Off Season— Active rest (August and September)
Weights 2-3 times a week
Jog and stretch daily
Active participation in other sports
(examples: volleyball, basketball)

General Fitness Tests— Test in early October and each month after during the season. It is best to test early in the week when the athlete's legs are fresh. Two attempts should be given with the best effort recorded for reference. Tests are standing start 50 yards in flats, standing long jump, standing start triple jump, and vertical jump.

Fall (October-December)

Long intervals of 660's-440's	Once a week
Short Intervals of 330's-150's	Once a week
2-3 mile run and hills	Once a week
Plyometric drills	Twice a week
Weights	2-3 times a week

In November start approach, technique work and curve 110's twice a week.

Early Season (January-March)

Weights	Twice a week
Technique jumping	Twice a week
Hills - Stairs	Once a week
Plyometrics	Twice a week
Curve 50's-100's	Twice a week
Short intervals	Twice a week
2 mile run	Once a week

In Season (April-June)

Weights	1-2 times a week
Technique Jumping	Twice a week
Plyometrics	Once a week (see notes on tapering this area)
Curve 50's	Twice a week
Short intervals	Twice a week

Sample Workouts:

Fall (October)
M—660-550-440, wts.
T—Plyometrics, 4 × 220's
W—6 × 330, wts.
TH—Plyometrics, 6 × 180's
F—2 mile run, 4 hills (300 yds long)
Weekend—Rest

Fall (November)

M—Plyometrics, 3 × 330
T—6 × curve 100's, jump, wts.
W—Plyometrics, 4 × 220
TH—see Tuesday
F—3 mile run, hills or stairs
Weekend—Rest

Early Season

    M—Plyometrics, 4 × 330
    T— 6 × curve 100's, jump, wts
    W—Plyometrics, 8 × 180
    TH—see Tuesday
    F—2 mile run, 7 × stairs or travel
    S—Meet or rest
    S—Rest

In Season

    M—Plyometrics, 6 × 180
    T— 6 × curve 50's, jump, wts.
    W—330-220-150-150-220-330
    TH—see Tuesday
    F—Jog-stretch-travel
    S—Meet
    S—Rest

DRILLS
Training

Examples of plyometric exercises are box depth jumps. Boxes should be 14''-18'' high to begin with. Variations can include jumping from one height box to the same height box off a double or single leg, off a low box to a higher one or a higher one to a lower one, or completely over the boxes landing on grass each time. Total recovery from these exercises range from 6-8 days, so the athlete needs to stop these 10-14 days before big meets. Other plyometric drills are hurdle hops off single and double legs, stair hops, bounding, a jump series of long jumps, triple jump, hop-hop-step-jump, 25 yd. hops off a single and double legs, hopping and bounding relays, high knee hops and skips, and rope jumping.

There is also a series of tests the West Germans use. These different groups are done at separate times. Group #1-5 standing hops off right and left legs, 5 hops from a 6 stride approach off each leg. Group #2-10 hurdle jumps off double leg, 5 hurdle jumps double leg, 10 hurdle jumps off take-off leg, 5 hurdle jumps off take-off leg, and 4 step approach scissors H.J. Group #3-10 1/2 or 1/4 squats with 50% max total time, 3 squats 70% max total time, 10 squats 60% max total time. In all these squats the thighs should be parallel to the floor. Group #4-30m sprint with a standing start, 150m sprint with a standing start. Group 5—technique analysis (approach, take-off, clearance).

Hurdle hops/jumps are an example
of plyometric exercises.

Technique

- Back rolls on high gym mats from a standing start or a trampoline.
- Back pull-overs with a partner for flexibility.
- Circle runs in the direction of the curve to sense what a true curve feels like, circle 8 runs.
- Mirror practice of double arm blocking and lead knee drive. This should also be walked and jogged through.
- Actual jumping (a) endurance training of up to 30 jumps, (b) technique training twice a week, 15-18 jumps each session and maximum jumping 10-15 jumps at PR heights regardless of misses.

Teaching Progression

- Determine the take-off foot—the athlete takes a running jump to see what foot is used to take off.
- Mark a curved approach on each side of the standard with tape.

- The athlete executes a scissors jump using a 5-step curved approach to a sitting landing position on the pit then a back landing position, and then a high back landing position.
- He/she then does a scissors jump as above working on a free knee drive up and across the body at take-off.
- The double arm action is started on the second to last step. For a right foot jumper, the left foot is forward on the second to last step and the right arm is back. The right arm is kept back as the athlete goes into the last step. The left arm then comes back naturally as the final step is taken. Both arms are now back and ready to punch upward. The hands should not go any higher than shoulder level at take-off.

FLEXIBILITY EXERCISES

Jog 880 mile, do these varied flexibility and other stretching exercises, stride 4-8 × 110's before the main workout. After the workout, the jumper should warm down with 440-880 jog of easy effort.

Hip Flexion

Purpose: To stretch upper hamstring.

- **Initial position:** Lying on the back with one leg kept straight and in firm contact with the floor.
- **Exercise:** The other knee is bent fully and the thigh is raised to as close to the chest as possible. While still pulling with the thigh muscles, an additional stretch is provided by grasping the knee with both hands and pulling slightly. The leg is then returned to the starting positon.
- Repeat for a total of 10 times.
- Repeat with the other leg.

Straight Leg Sit-Ups

Purpose: To stretch the low back.

- **Initial position:** Lying on back with arms across the chest or behind the head and legs secured.
- **Exercise:** Tuck the chin, raise the head and shoulders, then upper and lower back in a curling fashion as far as possible in one smooth motion, without twisting or turning, and return.
- Repeat for a total of 10 times.

Hip Flexion

Purpose: To stretch the hip flexors.
- **Initial position:** Back lying with one leg kept straight and in firm contact with the ground.
- **Exercise:** The other leg is raised, keeping the knee straight as far as possible. While still pulling the thigh muscles, an additional stretch is applied with the hands by grasping the thigh and pulling slightly. The leg then returns to the ground.
- Repeat for a total of 10 times.
- Repeat with the other leg.

Trunk Hyperextension

Purpose: To stretch trunk and dorsal spine.
- **Initial position:** Lie prone with arms at the sides and legs secrued.
- **Exercise:** Contract the back muscles and raise the head and shoulders being careful not to twist or turn.
- Repeat for a total of 5 times.

Heel Cord Stretch

Purpose: To stretch calf muscles.
- **Initial position:** Sitting on the floor with knee extended, ankle relaxed and a strap under the metatarsal arch.
- **Exercise:** Contract the muscle on the front of the lower leg, bringing the toe toward the shin. At the end of the range, keep contracting this muscle and pull the strap with the hands for additional stretch. Return to initial position.
- Repeat a total of 10 times.
- Repeat with other leg.

Hip Abduction

Purpose: To stretch thigh abductors and groin.
- **Initial position:** Side lying with the lower leg bent ninety degrees to aid in balance.
- **Exercise:** Raise the top leg straight up as high as possible and return, keeping the buttocks in and not allowing the leg to go in front or in back of the body.
- Repeat for a total of 10 times.
- Repeat lying on other side with other leg.

Hip Hyperextension

Purpose: To stretch the front thigh and hip flexors.
- **Initial position:** Lie prone with the knee of one leg flexed to approximately ninety (90) degree angle and grasp the ankle with the hand on the same side of the leg to be stretched.
- **Exercise:** Contract the muscles of the rear of the thigh and buttocks to raise the upper leg, keeping the leg from moving out or away from the body as it is raised guiding (not putting) with hand.
- Repeat for a total of 10 times
- Switch to the other leg and repeat.

Knee Flexion

Purpose: Increases the amount of flexion at a joint by breaking down adhesions and restoring extensibility to the various tissues of the joint.

- **Initial position:** prone position with the legs out straight.
- **Exercise:** The knee is bent and the lower leg is lifted through the range of motion as far as possible by itself. Then the ankle is grasped by the hand on the same side and the heel is brought down to touch the buttocks, being careful that the front of the hip does not lift up off the ground, then the leg returns to a straight position.
- Repeat for a total of 10 times.
- Repeat with other leg.

Foot Exercises

Purpose: For use in the regular warmup and/or rehabilitation.
- Plantar flexion and dorsiflexion
- Ankle rotations
- Arching of the foot
- Tendon stretch
- Heel raises
- Lateral stretch
- Resistance against a towel
- Marble pickup
- Towel gather
- Flexion and dorsiflexion against resistance
- Inversion and eversion against resistance
- Grip and spread toes

27
STRAIGHT LEAD LEG STRADDLE

Jesus Dapena
University of Iowa

Good high jumping requires a fast run-up, an efficient take-off, and a good drape over the bar. In this article, we shall describe techniques that will help straddle style jumpers to achieve these objectives.

TECHNIQUE IN THE LAST STRIDE OF THE RUN-UP

A high jumper's speed in the last stride of the run-up is important to the outcome of the jump. After planting the take-off foot, the horizontal velocity is reduced. Simultaneously, the quadriceps muscles of the take-off leg are stimulated by a stretch reflex, and the leg extends again, driving the jumper upward. Usually this is called, somewhat improperly the *transformation of horizontal velocity into vertical velocity*. Nevertheless, given a sufficiently strong leg and good take-off technique, the vertical velocity after take-off, and thus the peak height of the parabolic flight path of the center of gravity, will depend upon the horizontal velocity at the end of the run-up.

Straight Lead Leg Straddle

a   b   c   d   e   f   g

Diagram 1

At the start of the take-off the jumper's body should be relatively low, thus giving him a wide range of vertical motion, and ample time to push, before his take-off foot leaves the ground. For this reason the athlete should *gather* during the last stride, or better, during the last two strides. However, his body should neither go too low nor should it be dropping at the instant the take-off foot is planted.

The last phase of the action of the right leg (from now on we will refer to a jumper who takes off with his left foot), should be fluid and quick. There should be no braking of the momentum. The jumper's right foot should be placed on the ground softly, without a sound and as if the athlete is trying to *paw* the ground backward. Almost immediately after the right foot touches the ground, the jumper's hip should be above this foot, traveling forward, and his left knee should be catching up with his right knee (Diagram 1, positions a-c). His right leg should be flexed at about 100 to 110 degrees and retain that angle throughout the support phase and the following non-support phase, just prior to the take-off (Diagram 1, positions c-g). The jumper's right leg should push back with a progressive contraction of the right gluteus. The athlete should feel that his right leg is kneeling forward, with the knee approaching the ground. Thus, the hip is accelerated forward, leaving the shoulders behind. It should be emphasized that the jumper must try to make his hips go forward, not his shoulders backward. The athlete should also feel that he is traveling directly forward, with no upward or downward displacement. His right leg must be strong enough to support the entire weight of his body as shown in Diagram 1, positions d and e. These positions are not comfortable and require a strong right leg if the jumper's body is to be prevented from dropping. Specific strengthening exercises should be used in order to condition the leg for this important movement.

The movements described previously cause the hip flexors of the right leg to be stretched (Diagram 1, position f), thus stimulating a stretch reflex mechanism that initiates a strong kick of the right leg. The start of this action is shown in Diagram 1, positions f and g. Meanwhile, the jumper's left leg should have passed his right leg and extended forward to touch the ground as soon as possible.

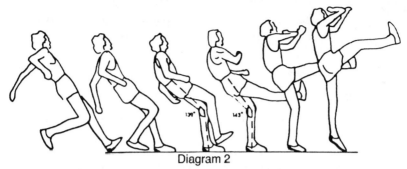

Diagram 2

If the technique of the last stride of the run-up is not perfect, the jumper's speed at the moment of touch-down for the take-off will be limited. Increasing the run-up speed is not the solution, because the faster the athlete runs, the more he will brake on the last supporting phase of the run-up, finishing at the same speed he would have had with a slower run-up. In addition, the strong deceleration experienced during the last stride will usually have a negative effect on the coordination of the entire jump. Thus, an improvement of the technique of the last stride is necessary before increasing the speed of the run-up.

RHYTHM

Apart from velocity, rhythm in the last strides of the run-up is important. Rhythm in the last strides should be: pom...pom...pom...pomPOM. The tempo should be fastest in the last stride. This increase in rhythm is independent of the velocity of the jumper. To obtain it, the athlete should try to bring his left foot forward even before his right foot makes contact with the ground. He should then, in a fast and continuous movement, straighten his left leg as his hip goes forward, and place his left foot on the ground, ahead of his body. The athlete should feel that his left foot makes contact with the ground immediately after the right foot. However, he should not achieve this at the expense of a decrease in the separation of his thighs at the end of the supporting phase (Diagram 1, position f). A fluid backward pawing of the ground with the right foot will help rhythm as well as velocity.

This change in rhythm has been found to be effective in practice, although no mechanical explanation has been found. It has been suggested, however, that the change in rhythm might act as a neuromuscular stimulant.

TAKE-OFF LEG

After the plant, the take-off leg should not be allowed to bend to any extent. Contraction provoked by the stretch reflex on the quadriceps muscles of the take-off leg is believed to work most efficiently when the leg bends no farther than 140 degrees (Diagram 2). Thus, the take-off leg should be tense when it is planted on the ground, and the jumper should try to keep it stiff and almost straight throughout the take-off, with an especially strong effort at the end. The leg will, of course, bend, but not too much. It will spring back to its straight position, causing the jumper to leave the ground.[1]

FREE LIMB ACTION

While the leg bends in the first part of the take-off, the arms and free leg should be thrown forward and upward vigorously, thus increasing the force exerted on the ground. Floppers usually make a weak thrust with the free limbs, relying mainly on the acceleration of the trunk produced by the extension of the take-off leg. Straddlers, on the other hand, usually accelerate their free limbs upward more forcefully, accelerating the trunk later by a transfer of momentum from the limbs, and a weaker extension of the take-off leg. Different techniques with the free limbs, intermediate between those described previously, are also frequent, especially in the case of floppers. It is not known which is the optimum technique, and if there is such an optimum, it might well be a different optimum for each jumper.

FORCES AND TORQUES

During the take-off the jumper exerts a force on the ground. The ground reacts, exerting on the athlete a force that accelerates his body upward. If this reaction force passes throught the center of gravity of the athlete, the jumper's angular momentum does not change. In high jumping the force does not normally pass through the center of gravity of the athlete and the torque thus generated produces a change in his angular momentum. In other words, the body of the athlete is forced to rotate. Rotation is necessary for bar clearance. This type of force is called an eccentric force. Eccentric forces, however, cannot be as strong as forces that pass through the center of gravity; therefore, the athlete should make the line of action of the force pass as near to his center of gravity as possible.

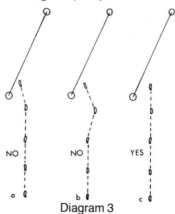

Diagram 3

Most straddlers have a tendency to lean excessively toward the bar during the take-off in order to increase the torque. The direction of the last strides of the run-up can have an influence on the degree of body lean during the take-off. It is not unusual for straddlers to follow a curve in their last one or two strides (Diagram 3, positions a and b). This 1) contributes to lean during the take-off, 2) is usually associated with a diagonal upward and action to the left of the lead leg, which frequently dislodges the bar on the way up, and 3) can be a source of injuries to the take-off knee and ankle. Steps should be kept perfectly in line (Diagram 3, position c), and the jumper's body should lean toward the bar as little as possible.

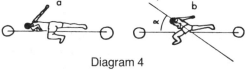

Diagram 4

DIAGONAL DIVE STRADDLE

Straddle bar clearance techniques can be divided into: 1) *parallel,* in which the longitudinal axis of the trunk is parallel to the bar (Diagram 4, position a), and 2) *diagonal,* in which it makes an angle with the bar when seen from above (Diagram 4, position b). We can also distinguish between dive and non-dive jumps, the *divers* having their shoulders lower than their hips at the peak of the jump.

I believe that the diagonal dive staddle is the best straddle technique, because a smaller lean is required toward the bar at take-off and a better drape at the peak of the jump is allowed. In the diagonal dive straddle, the layout is obtained less by leaning toward the bar and more by a checking of linear motion, similar to the one reported to occur in the flop.[2] This checking makes the jumper feel as though he is somersaulting forward (Diagram 5). Of

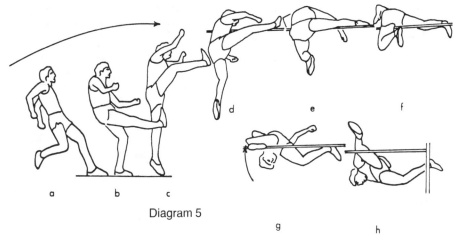

Diagram 5

Illustrations 1-5. In the penultimate stride (Illustration 1), Knoedel has a speed between 20.7 and 22.3 ft./sec. The support phase on his right leg is not very fluid. His right foot is too far forward and passive, instead of pawing back, when it makes contact with the ground. Knoedel's gather is excessive. His right knee does not go forward and downward fast enough. The hip lags behind most of the time. His entire right leg acts as a brake. After the hip passes the vertical through the right foot, his right leg does not push back very hard due to the contraction of the right gluteus. By the time his right foot loses contact with the ground (Illustration 4) his speed has dropped to 18.7 — 19.0 ft./sec., which is very slow. Straddlers who have good technique reach speeds of about 23 ft./sec. Illustrations 5-7. The action of Knoedel's take-off leg is excellent in this jump. Although not shown in the sequence, the minimum knee angle, shortly before Illustration 6 is 142°, and then Knoedel extends his take-off leg well. He uses a strong lead leg and double arm action. His lean to the left is slightly too marked. Illustrations 7-12. Knoedel's left knee is pulled up quickly and correctly, going toward his left shoulder (Illustrations 7-9). His right arm goes down (Illustrations 8 and 9) and then swings back hard (Illustrations 9-12). This forces his trail leg to swing up in the opposite direction and clear the bar (Illustrations 10-12). Overall, the bar clearance is good. It can be seen that the right arm is pulled back too late, and thus, although the rotation of the leg is fast because of the strong backward swing of the arm, the trail leg is not raised in time, and would dislodge the bar (Illustration 11) if it were higher. Knoedel's right arm should be sent back earlier, even if it is at the cost of some loss in the range of movement.

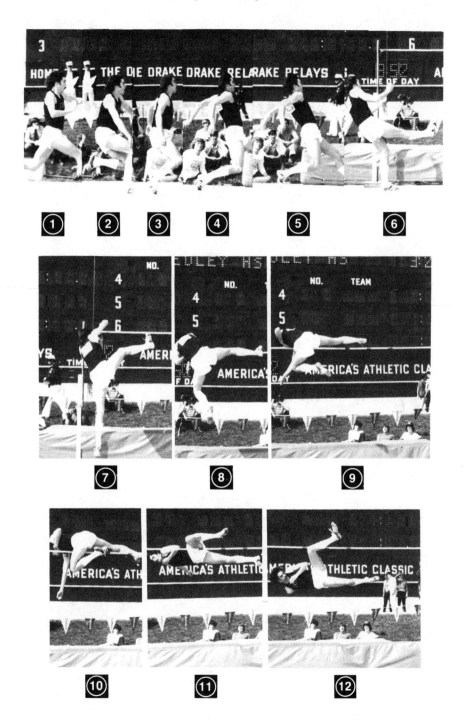

course, he does not somersault forward perfectly. He is also leaning somewhat to the left, and the final result is a hybrid between a parallel straddle and a somersault. If the jumper is an experienced straddler, he should feel that he is jumping upward and slightly forward instead of upward and slightly to the left. He should not feel that he is jumping to the left at all. An emphasis on checking the linear motion is recommended only for straddlers who use a straight lead leg; straddlers who use a bent lead leg could have problems. After leaving the ground, the jumper should lift his take-off knee

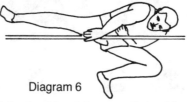

Diagram 6

quickly toward his left shoulder (Diagram 6). In this way, the rotation produced by the checking of linear motion in the take-off (clockwise in Diagram 5, position a-c) helps the trail leg clear the bar (also a clockwise rotation in Diagram 5, positions e-h), and Diagram 7.

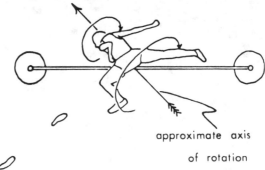

approximate axis

of rotation

Diagram 7

After take-off in the diagonal dive straddle, the jumper should be going in the same direction he was going in the run-up. Thus, the place on the pit where his hips fall should be in line or almost in line with the run-up, and not to the left (Diagram 8).

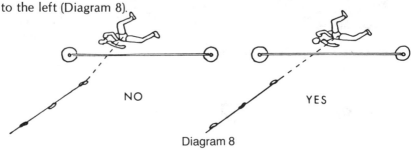

NO   YES

Diagram 8

Once the jumper leaves the ground, the angular momentum that he carries is not in itself sufficient to allow him to clear the bar. In addition, he must execute a series of compensatory movements,[3] the most important being a lowering of the head and trunk (Diagram 9, position a-d), a lowering (Diagram 9, position a) and then raising the right arm quickly (Diagram 9, position a-e).

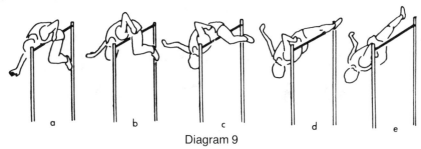

Diagram 9

References

1. Ozolin, Nikolay, "The High Jump Take-Off Mechanism, *Track Technique* No. 52, 1973 pp. 1668-1671.

2. Ecker, Tom, "Track and Field Dynamics" (Los Altos, Calif, *Tafnews Press,* 1971), pp. 64-67.

3. Dapena, Jesus, "Searching for the Best Straddle Technique," *Track Technique* No. 55, 1974 pp. 1753-1756.

28

THE HIGH JUMP STYLE OF RON JOURDAN

Jimmy Carnes and Don Hester
University of Florida

Ron Jourdan of the University of Florida proved to be the most consistent of the 7-foot jumpers over the past indoor and outdoor season. His dominance over the 7-foot barrier continues as the 1970 indoor season begins. Ron's first place efforts of 7 feet at the Liberty Bowl in Memphis, Tennessee, and at the Orange Bowl invitational at Miami, Florida should give due warning of another outstanding year for this product of the University of Florida.

Over the 1969 indoor-outdoor season, Ron cleared varying heights of 7 feet or over 25 times with a best jump of 7 feet, 2 inches. He narrowly missed a new American indoor record of 7 feet, 3½ inches on two occasions. On one of these attempts, the crossbar did not fall until Jourdan had walked back to pick up his sweat suit.

Jourdan is dedicated to his event. He completes each day's workout in a conscientious, methodical fashion. He is convinced that a thorough weight-training program was and still is essential to his success. Ron is a senior this year, majoring in the College of Physical Education and Health. Standing 6 feet, 1 inch and weighing 165 pounds, he blends power, jumping technique, and a strong competitive attitude into a winning combination.

The accompanying illustrations which show the jumping style of Ron Jourdan were taken during actual competition at 7 feet, 1 inch during the 1969 NCAA Outdoor Championship Meet in Knoxville, Tennessee.

The High Jump Style of Ron Jourdan

THE APPROACH

Illustrations 1, 2, and 3. Utilizing an angle of 27°, Ron starts his approach run from an ititial check mark with two walking steps (the walking steps and a portion of the approach are not shown). Transition from the walk into the approach run is smooth with a consistent increase in speed throughout the run. From Illustration 1 to Illustration 2 Ron's eyes have shifted from watching a second check mark to focusing on the crossbar. Illustration 3 shows the preliminary movement of the arms outward and to the side, which aids in lateral body balance.

THE TAKE-OFF

Illustrations 4, 5, and 6. In Illustration 4, Ron's arms are in an extended position to the rear, subsequent to their use in a forceful swinging reach upward. The take-off leg is extended for its heel-to-toe foot plant while the kicking or lead leg is in a bent position recovering from the final approach stride. Illustration 5 shows a powerful straight lead leg kick in coordination with an upward arm thrust by both arms, placing ultimate pressure on the take-off leg. The bend at the knee of the take-off leg will be no greater than is shown in Illustration 5. Backward body lean, which is necessary, is not easily detected in Illustrations 4 and 5 because of camera angle. In Illustration 6, the take-off foot and leg have finished their explosive extension. The lead foot and arms continue to extend toward the crossbar. Notice Jourdan's lead leg is slightly bent at this time but becomes straight once again over the crossbar.

CROSSBAR CLEARANCE

Illustrations 7, 8, 9, and 10. Illustration 7 shows the start of crossbar clearance. Ron's lead arm has reached over the crossbar. His head and lead foot are close to the apex of the jumper's flight path or trajectory and his torso has been turned toward the crossbar. Rotation was initiated from the ground. This was accomplished through a combination of eccentric thrust (a force applied indirectly under the center of gravity) by utilizing a slight lean toward the crossbar at take-off, a turning of the hips toward the crossbar as the outside or kicking leg reaches its apex, and by a placement or pivoting of the take-off foot toward the crossbar at the foot plant and take-off.

Illustration 8 shows a continuation of rotation as the lead arm and head drop to a lower position on the pit side of the crossbar, resulting in a modified dive straddle clearance. The trail leg is being brought up and assumes a position with approximately a 90° bend at the knee. Illustration 9 shows clearly the reason for naming this type of clearance the straddle.

We instruct a jumper to continue his normal rotational speed while he is over the crossbar with a conscious lifting of the trail leg and maintain it in a bent position at the knee. Ron's right arm moves upward as shown in Illustrations 9 and 10. We feel this is a resultant action to lifting the trail leg and is involuntary. We do not teach a lifting of the right arm.

It will be noticed in Illustration 10 that on this particular jump the normal body rotation over the crossbar was inhibited by the lead foot appearing to be caught in mid-air and remaining in a position near crossbar height instead of reaching down toward the pit as it should. This made the trail leg clearance more difficult and caused the trail leg to be straightened unnecessarily.

THE LANDING

Illustrations 11 and 12. Illustrations 11 and 12 show a normal landing procedure for the straddle technique when landing in a soft pit.

It is our feeling that success in the high jump event is achieved through securing jumpers who possess physical potential with attitudes for achievement, through an effective weight-training program, personal observation and correction of jumping techniques, and utilization of the mechanical principles involved.

29
VAULTING ANALYZED

Jim Santos
California State University

When analyzing film, it is important that the coach or athlete be able to interpret the body mechanics of the event. In the pole vault, it becomes even more complex, because not only must the body mechanics be analyzed, but the movement of the pole adds another dimension to the event.

As the films are broken down for analysis, the viewer must be aware of several areas of concentration in the vault:
- The plant.
- The angle of the pole on the plant.
- Displacement of the center of mass as the vaulter goes into the take-off and rock-back.
- The pull-up and bar clearance.

KEY POINTS TO WATCH FOR
IN THE PLANT
- The vaulter must try to develop the largest angle possible between the pole and the runway at take-off.
- A high plant with the top hand should be used.
- There should be no pulling with the arms until the turn.
- The vaulter's head should be kept in line with the body throughout the vault.
- The take-off foot should be directly under the top hand.

Vaulting Analyzed

On the plant, the angle of the pole is approximately 45 degrees (Illustration 1). Porter shows excellent plant position for the pole with his right arm extended well over his head and directly over his left take-off foot.

As shown in Illustration 2, the vaulter has not maintained a strong left arm, and has allowed it to collapse on the plant. He has also allowed his head and shoulders to shift to the left of the pole and out of the line of trajectory that should have afforded him his greatest force into the pole. His right knee is in good position as he is driving into the pole.

After the take-off (Illustration 3), notice how Porter's upper body has drifted to the left side of the pole, and his head is not in line with his right hand. He has maintained good leg separation at this point by keeping his left leg back.

The Hinge Moment Principle is coming into full effect now (Illustration 4) as Porter has a great right arm extension from the pole. His right leg has continued to move as it remains bent, and is curling back into his body. His left leg is doing a great deal of work as he is trying to get it to swing through and up.

As shown in Illustration 5, Porter's right knee has curled back almost to his face, with his left leg still maintaining force to add to his rock-back position.

Porter maintains good rock-back position by keeping his head in line with his spine (Illustration 6). At this point, his greatest asset is the fact that he has not allowed his head to drop back, which would have forced his legs down and into the bar. He is also forcing his knees to come back as far as possible into his body in order to shorten the radius of his legs, and thus increase the speed of the rock-back.

In the rock-back (Illustration 7), Porter has allowed his lower body to come back into the pole so that his feet are almost directly over his head before he initiates his pull-up.

On the pull-up, the vaulter maintained position with his head by not allowing it to drop back (Illustration 8). His legs are in good position because they are pointed directly up over his head. However, Porter has lost a great deal of power due to the fact that he allowed his body and center of mass to drift away from the pole. The vaulter's right arm should not be in the mid-line of his body with the pole, but should be on the right side of his body. His left arm has to follow the same line of direction as the pole bends; consequently, he will have a rather inefficient pull-up through the pole.

Illustration 9 shows poor position for a powerful pull-up as the vaulter's body and center of mass are completely out of line with the pole. His left forearm is not able to apply any pressure on the pole for stability, and his right arm loses its pulling force by having to pull down the side of the pole. At this point, Porter must have the feeling of controlling the pole as he rotates off the top hand.

Notice the angle of the pole on release (Illustration 10). Due to his poor take-off, Porter was not able to make the correction on the vault; therefore, his power on this vault was not as efficient and as strong as it could have been.

In Illustration 11 Porter shows good bar clearance position with his legs flexed back, and his thumbs turned in.

As shown in Illustration 12, Porter's arms lift only after his chest has cleared the bar.

Illustration 1 shows Tracanelli running in a good upright position with the pole held close to his side. These two factors aid in his drive towards the box. His pole is held just above head height and he shows good concentration for the plant.

Tracanelli has a good high plant but he has not moved the pole out in front enough to get the full advantage of powering into it (Illustration 2). Notice that the angle formed by the pole and his body is somewhat less than 45 degrees indicating a slight backward lean at the plant. This position may cause some energy to be lost down the shaft of the pole.

The plant is very high as Tracanelli drives hard into the pole (Illustration 3). He shows good extension of the take-off leg and it is well to notice full plantar flexion of the foot exhibiting maximum effort in the drive. His right knee drive is excellent and his bottom arm effectively keeps his body from moving into the pole at take-off.

As shown in Illustration 4, Tracanelli continues to drive into the pole staying well behind it. This position can be attributed to his bottom arm again, controlling the body behind the pole.

Tracanelli begins his rock-back as the pole reaches maximum bend (Illustration 5). Notice how effectively he uses the bottom arm. He initiates his rock-back behind the pole, which helps keep the energy in it during this phase of the vault. His head position is excellent staying in line with the spine.

Illustration 6 shows the vaulter's head maintaining alignment with his spine very well in the cradle position. At this point, the take-off leg has caught up with the lead leg and Tracanelli begins to shift more of his body weight toward his shoulders while staying behind the pole.

Tracanelli begins to lift his hips above his shoulders (Illustration 7). However, notice the position of his head. He appears to be looking for the bar by raising his head slightly. This may affect the positioning of his center of gravity causing it to shift slightly forward in the direction of the pole. At the same time Tracanelli is able to overcome this by flexing his knees to keep the center of mass in line with his bottom arm, thus aiding in staying behind the pole.

Illustration 8 shows that Tracanelli's center of gravity has shifted forward ahead of the pole. His head is flexed more towards his chest. However, his feet and hips are high and his shoulders are maintained behind the pole contributing to his vertical lift.

At this point, Tracanelli has started his pull (Illustration 9). Notice the pull is down the shaft of the pole and through the hip of his outside leg while the vaulter attempts to keep his head behind the pole. This action helps keep his legs from dropping on the crossbar and enhances vertical lift due to the return of energy from the pole.

As he completes his turn, Tracanelli continues to drive his right leg, which aids in keeping both legs up. His bottom hand has detached and Tracanelli continues to drive down the pole shaft with his top hand to enhance his vertical lift (Illustration 10).

Tracanelli releases the pole and explodes off the top of it over the bar (Illustration 11). He has assumed a rather flat-out position over the bar, which would not work well at higher bar heights. Notice his straight legs. This lends to a quicker dropping action of the body on the bar. Slight flexion of the lower leg would have kept the body up longer enabling greater passing distance behind the bar.

Illustration 12 shows Tracanelli dropping on the bar very fast because his legs have dropped below chest level.

The vaulter remains relaxed and does not rush over the bar (Illustration 13). He completes clearance by raising the elbow of his right arm high and turning the thumb of his right hand down. This action aids in keeping the elbows in line with the body and in keeping the chest in.

After a successful bar clearance (Illustration 14). Tracanelli descends in a near vertical direction as if he were going to land on his feet. However, notice that his left leg flexes and his arms remain raised high to control the rate of backward rotation coming off the bar.

Finally, Tracanelli prepares for contact with the pit after completing enough rotation to place him on his lower back, thus allowing for the greatest absorption of energy from his vertical descent (Illustration 15).

In his preparation for the pole plant, Lipscomb has started to move the pole out in front of his body (Illustration 1).

As his take-off foot (left foot) is planted, Lipscomb's top hand is directly over the plant foot (Illustration 2). However, at this moment he has not extended his right arm high enough over his head; therefore, his plant is considered poor for the proper take-off. Lipscomb's left arm is in good position, because he has not extended the pole over his head. The pole is only at an approximate 33 degree angle, which is a most difficult position from which to take off on the vault.

Because as shown in the previous illustration the vaulter had a low plant, and low angle of pole, he does not have the leverage in which to apply pressure into the pole with his left arm. Notice at this point (Illustration 3) how the left arm has completely collapsed and has allowed his center of mass to shift forward, almost under his left hand. Lipscomb has good leg separation with his driving leg in good position to allow for the storing of energy into the pole.

As shown in Illustration 4, the vaulter's left leg has come up too fast, which forced him into an early rock-back position. At this point, Lipscomb should have delayed his left leg, and kept it back more, developing a greater separation between his legs. Because his left leg has started to move forward, he is forced into rocking back early, and loses the force developed by the Hinge Moment Principle.

Illustration 5 shows that the vaulter's right knee has drawn back well, reducing the radius of the leg allowing him to go into a rock-back position at a faster rate of speed. His left leg is now starting to catch up with his right leg as he rocks back. Lipscomb has done a good job keeping away from the pole because his right arm is straight.

In the rock-back position shown in Illustratioin 6, the vaulter's left leg has now caught up to his right knee. Both legs are now flexed at an angle of approximately 70 degrees looking at the angle developed from the hip to the left knee.

The rock-back is not complete at this point (Illustration 7), because Lipscomb's knees are not directly over his head. As he initiates his pull, he will not be pulling straight up into the pole, due to the fact that his hips are not back far enough into his body.

Initiating the pull-up (Illustration 8), Lipscomb has placed his arms in good position. His left arm is inside the pole, and he has maintained leverage and pulling power with his right arm by not starting to pull too soon. The fault in this position is that the vaulter has let his hip drift away from the pole, and as he initiates the pull-up, he will not be pulling straight up, but shall instead pull into the bar.

Illustration 9 shows that the vaulter has initiated his pull, and is going into the bar on the pull-up.

Lipscomb has maintained contact with the pole, which is good for stability on top of the bar (Illustration 10). However, he still has momentum going up, and by keeping his right hand on the pole, he gets his final drive off the pole.

Illustration 11 shows excellent jackknife position with the hips high, thumbs turned in, and vaulter's right leg still up to keep his hips up.

Still maintaining the jackknife position with the thumbs turned in, the vaulter allows his own rotation to aid in bar clearance (Illustration 12). His arms are in good position, and must not be raised at this point to clear the bar, because his movement will force the chest into the bar.

Upon bar clearance with the chest, the vaulter's arms are raised slightly to clear the bar (Illustration 13).

By raising his arms, Lipscomb has slowed his rotation back, allowing him to fall into the pit safely (Illustration 14).

Illustration 15 shows the rotation slowed greatly, and the landing is safe as Lipscomb's body will absorb most of the shock from his fall.

ON THE SWING
- The top hand acts as the Hinge Moment Principle application, and is the axis of rotation.
- The top arm should remain fully extended.
- The take-off leg should be fully extended.
- The drive knee should be flexed.
- The head should remain in line with the spine and not drop back.

ON THE ROCK-BACK POSITION
- The take-off leg should catch up to the driving knee.
- Shorten the radius by drawing the knees into the body.
- Elevate the hips above the head.

BAR CLEARANCE
- Do not throw the arms back.
- Keep the head down, which prevents the chest from hitting the bar.
- Keep the thumbs turned in.

As film analysis is used, the knowledge of body mechanics becomes more important as the coach or athlete attempts to determine strengths or faults. Without question the use of film is a great aid to coaching and improvement in sports movement, and becomes an ever-increasing tool for success in track and field.

The acompanying pictures taken at the NCAA Championships in Austin, Texas last June show the winner, Ed Lipscomb of Oregon State, with a vault of 17'-3" (Series A); third place finisher, Francois Tacenelli of UCLA, with a vault of 17'-0" (Series B); and the sixth place finisher, Terry Porter of Kansas, who vaulted 16'-8" (Series C); I am indepted to my vault coach, Ed Otter, for his help in analyzing the vaulting form of these three excellent vaulters.

Proper conditioning techniques will enable a vaulter to achieve his/her true potential.

30

AN OFF-SEASON TRAINING AND CONDITIONING PROGRAM FOR HIGH SCHOOL POLE VAULTERS

Robert N. McKie
Villa Park, California, High School

Track coaches will generally agree that the pole vault is one of the most technical of all track and field events. A young athlete who is considering this event must realize that many years (probably 6 to 8) of training and competing are necessary before he can expect to be a competent vaulter. Not only proficiency in the many movements of the vault itself are necessary, but general conditioning, improvement of speed, better body control, and greater upper body strength are all areas to which he must give his attention. The implication is clear. If he is to be successful in the pole vault, the high school athlete will have to devote some time in the off-season to personal improvement in the previously mentioned areas.

In this article the aspects of training and conditioning of a high school vaulter during his off-season will be discussed. The definition of off-season depends somewhat on several factors: 1) the length and time of year of the school's outdoor season; 2) whether or not there is indoor competition and the time and length of that season; 3) whether or not the vaulter competes during the summer on a regular basis; and 4) the length of time during the year he desires to compete and/or has the opportunity to do so. A high school vaulter's season of competition may be further limited by such factors as weather and the facilities (indoor and out) available to him for practice.

During the past three track seasons, we have had the privilege of working with two fine vaulters, Keith Schommel and Tim Vahlstrom. They both achieved high school all-American status in their senior year, with best marks of 16 feet, 3¼ inches and 16 feet, 1 inch. Their training programs will be used as our criteria. Out definition of off-season will be roughly from the end of June until early January.

We think it is important for vaulters and all track and field participants at the high school level to have a short period of time away from training and competition each year. That period might be anywhere from two weeks to two months, but a break in training is needed in order to begin again with a fresh mental outlook.

The off-season training and conditioning program can be broken down into four parts: 1) running; 2) weight training; 3) gymnastics; and 4) vaulting and/or plant drills.

Overview. As our conditioning program is resumed, probably in late July, the time will be fairly equally divided between distance running and weight training. Weight training sessions will be held three days a week, with two or three days of running. This training will continue throughout the off-season. Distance workouts will be continued for seven to eight weeks, running four to five days a week for the last four weeks instead of two or three days. Emphasis will gradually shift to sprint work by early October. One day a week of distance running will still be included in the workouts through the end of the off-season. Gymnastic workouts will be included two days a week in the months of October, November, December, January, and on into the early outdoor season. Plant drills and running with the pole may be worked in once or twice a week in the months of October through January. Some actual practice vaults may be taken every two or three weeks during this same period. If there is to be indoor competition in January and/or February, then the frequency of vaulting will naturally be increased in December and January.

Running. When off-season training is resumed in late June or early July, we begin easily. During the first three or four weeks, the distance runs will cover only two or three miles over varying terrain. Once or twice during this early period, the vaulters run four or five miles. All of this is done at an easy pace to build endurance and increase aerobic capacity. The number of days per week they work out during this period would be five or six. Because of the proximity of hills in our area, hill running is worked in once or twice a week. Usually it will be just a run through the hills, but occasionally it might be a few repeat runs of 300 to 400 yards up a steep hill. Workouts with the cross-country team can be included as an occasional change of pace for the vaulters.

In illustration 1, Keith Schimmel shows good body, pole alignment just prior to take-off.

While his take-off position is good, it is not perfect. Notice the high pole plant. The top arm position indicates a slightly late plant (Illustration 2).

As shown in Illustration 3, the lead knee is driven up well. Keith's upper body

indicates a correct swing from the shoulders position.

Illustration 4 shows that Keith's trail leg has not caught up with his lead leg, aiding the raising of his hips.

In Illustration 5, Keith shows excellent rock-back position. His back is flat, his feet are close to the top of the pole, and his hips are behind the pole and rising. The position of his arms indicates he is waiting in rock-back position.

Keith has timed his rotation and pull quite well with the straightening of the pole. Notice the good hip position with his body vertical (Illustration 6).

Illustrations 7 and 8 show that he has gotten away from his pole a little early, causing a less smooth than desired bar clearance.

A good arch style clearance (Illustrations 9 and 10) shows that Keith has recovered well from the error mentioned in Illustrations 7 and 8.

Realizing that the top of the vault was not quite correct, Keith looks down to prepare himself for landing (Illustration 11).

Notice that Keith will not land in the center of the pit, indicating a loss of alignment somewhere in the vault (Illustration 12).

Overdistance running of three to five miles will continue through September and October. Acutally, there need not be a set time when a change-over to short interval running takes place. Rather, when we feel that our vaulters have sufficient overdistance background (six to eight weeks), then short interval running can be interspaced with distance runs. By November, however, the vaulters will be into short running almost entirely. An example of a week's running schedule for early November is as follows:

Monday: Three to 4 miles easy running in the hills.

Wednesday: Jog one-half mile; 6 × 150 yards on the track at seven-eighths speed. Job 290 yards between each.

Friday: Jog one-half mile; 16 × 110 yards on the grass at three-quarters speed. Walk back each time.

Sunday: Jog a mile on the grass; do a series of short sprints on the runway at three-quarters speed. Walk 220 between.

Other variations in our running during November, December, and January might include 1) running with the pole (30 to 40 yards at a time); 2) step-up/step-down sprint workout, consisting of 110, 220, 330, 440 yards and then back down again; 3) a mile circuit run (repeated two or three times) which includes sit-ups, pull-ups, push-ups, hurdle stretching; 4) 3 × 440 yards at three-quarters speed with a two-minute interval; and 5) repeat runs of 500 to 600 yards up a fairly steep hill.

Weight-Training. We feel that there is no substitute for weight training for the high school vaulter. We want him to do it all through the off-season, beginning at least in September, and continuing until midway through the competitive season (probably late March). He might then drop it completely or limit his workouts to one or two a week. We would prefer to have him drop weight training completely at this point.

During the months that the athlete is doing weight training, he will have three workouts a week. Training sessions might last one to two hours, depending on the amount of time the boy has available. To try to do the workout in less than 45 minutes, however, would be inadequate for the necessary benefits to accrue.

Our basic weight workout consists of three sets of 10 repetitions of nearly all the exercises included in the workout. The vaulter works with the amount of weight he can lift 10 times, but only with some degree of difficulty. Some power sets (3 to 5 repetitions) may also be included.

The make-up of a typical weight training session is as follows: 1. Warm-up. 2. Bench press on the weight machine. 3. Incline bench press with a barbell. 4. Flies with dumbbells. 5. Lat pulls on the machine. 6. Curls with a dumbbell alternating the arms. 7. Sit-ups and leg lifts on an incline board. 8. Leg press on the machine. 9. Toe raises on the machine. 10. Overhead pull-overs with a barbell.

Gymnastics. These two workouts during the week would usually last one and one-half to two hours. Sometimes they would follow a distance run or sprint workout, and occasionally would take the place of the running. The workout consists of routinely doing three sets of 10 repetitions of gymnastics exercises as follows:

High Bar. 1. Pull-ups. 2. Pull-overs without touching the bar. 3. Rock-backs (hanging, bring the legs straight up next to the bar, pulling the hips up over the bar). 4. Kip-ups.

Rope. Climb 3 or 5 times with the legs straight, using long arm reaches on the rope.

Rings. 1. Muscle-ups. 2. Swinging into rock-back and handstand positions.

Parallel Bars. 1. Bar dips. 2. Mounts and dismounts.

Stall Bars. Leg lifts.

Tumbling. 1. Backward roll into a handstand position. 2. Walking on the hands. 3. Handstand push-ups.

Vaulting/Vault Drills. In order for a young vaulter to become proficient in this difficult event, it is necessary for him to vault more than just during the outdoor season, which would be three to four months long. An additional two to three months of indoor competition and practice would improve the situation. He must do actual vaulting at least part of the off-season, so that he is not starting over each year when the season officially begins.

There are certain obstacles which might make it difficult for the high school pole vaulter to practice during the off-season: 1) Weather conditions might not permit outdoor practice and the indoor facilities are not available or limited. 2) Interscholastic rules may prohibit organized practice after school during the off-season. This would not constitute a problem for runners, or even shot putters, who can usually find a facility on which to practice on their own, but the pole vaulter will rarely find readily available the pits, standards, poles, etc., needed to practice.

If they are able to overcome these obstacles, we would have our high school vaulters do actual vaulting once every two weeks during late summer and fall. Then for six weeks before regular season practice begins, they might vault once a week. These vaulting sessions could be without a crossbar at least half the time, the emphasis being on the run, plant, and getting off the ground properly.

Finally, we would have them take short runs with the pole on the runway or on the track, completing the run by simulating the shifting of the pole forward and passing it overhead for the plant. Without having any pits or standards available, they could do plant drills. This time would be well spent if they simply drilled on the last three to four steps of the run, moving the pole forward and up into the plant position, then driving off the take-off leg, jumping just slightly off the runway. This would be repeated many times to develop the feel and timing of the pole shift, a high plant, and proper body position under the top arm.

31

CONDITIONING A VAULTER

John Pappa and Bill LaQuard
University of California, Davis

Pole vaulting has become a very interesting event at the various levels of competition. Due to a trend toward upgrading track programs, an increase in better performers at the junior high and high school levels has resulted. The instruction or coaching of mechanics received by a pole vaulter at an early age helps prepare him for participation as a collegiate athlete. Mechanically speaking, most vaulters have been able to master the fiber glass pole effectively.

Due to the lack of well-defined objective tests to determine the potential of an individual, general observation by the coach must serve this purpose. In addition, many coaches may feel that a vaulter has the physical ability to perform better, but does not because of inadequate conditioning. Improvement which is the result of practicing continuously on the mechanics of form is as important as a conditioning program. This practice will prepare the athlete physically and mentally to cope with his particular event.

A coach must consider the development and maturity of an athlete during his years of competition. This is an added ingredient for better performance, although many athletes do not improve but remain in a static-type position.

For the past five years vaulting has presented a stimulating challenge to us. A great of material has been written on the mechanics of fiber glass vaulting. After study and experience in working with vaulters during this time, it is our feeling that more than just mechanics are required to develop a top vaulter during his career. Conditioning of the vaulter's body to prepare him to meet an obstacle which is a challenge is necessary.

During the past several years, we have had two former junior college vaulters who made significant improvement while at Davis. Steve Sanders from Sunland vaulted 13 feet before entering Davis, and improved to 15 feet while placing fifth in the 1967 NCAA College Division Championships. George Newstrom from Hartnell vaulted 13 feet, 6 inches in 1967 before entering Davis. During the 1968 season, George vaulted 15 feet, 4 inches and placed second in the NCAA College Division Championships. It is our feeling that the conditioning program these two vaulters participated in contributed significantly to their exceptional rate of improvement and success while here.

We had other vaulters during this time who lacked the discipline to participate in the conditioning program and made very little improvement.

The conditioning program that was used with both Sanders and Newstrom consists primarily of gymnastic exercises. It was started in January, but previously during the fall quarters the vaulters enrolled in a regular tumbling and gymnastics class, which gave them a basic background and prepared them for the special program.

The program is set up primarily to exercise and develop the major muscle groups of the body, including the lower back, stomach, hips, legs, and the shoulder gridle. It does not involve barbells or dumbbells but features the use of medicine balls as part of the training to obtain more explosiveness of the muscles and joints. High bars and uneven bars are also used for pull-ups and lay-out circles to help flexibility. Rings and horses are also used. All of these are intermediary-isometric exercises.

Each conditioning workout begins with the vaulter running around the perimeter of the gymnasium floor. Mats are placed at 30-yard intervals. The vaulter runs at a relaxed pace and upon reaching the mat performs a forward roll without changing his pace. He does four or five laps around the gymnasium before starting his next exercise, which is jumping in place, and this is done with emphasis on pushing up with the toes. During this one-minute drill the arms change from side movement to upward movement. Following a 10-second rest period, the ankles are exercised. A foot roll (rocking from heel to toe with the knees bending as the vaulter rocks on his toes) is used for the ankles.

The knee strengthening exercise follows the ankle exercise. Sitting on the floor in a tuck position, with his arms grasping his knees, the vaulter exerts pressure forward. Pressure is exerted for a 10-second count.

Exercises for the quadriceps and stomach muscles are next. From a long-sitting position, and leaning backwards slightly, the vaulter's legs are extended and lifted approximately 8 inches off the ground. His arms are held out to the side for balance. This is done for a 10-second count. Then the legs are held at the same position and a circular motion is executed with the legs together. Ten repetitions.

The next exercise is the pike. From a supine position with the arms at the sides, the vaulter's legs are brought over the top of his body and extended in back of his shoulder 20 times. This is followed by a knee and back exercise in which the athlete is standing in a tuck position. His hands are placed on the floor in front of his feet. Then he straightens his knees to assume a pike position. Ten of these are done in a set.

The cat push-up is next. This exercise is ideal for strengthening the hips, shoulder, ankle, wrists, and arms. The athlete assumes a push-up position with a high bridge (hips up high). His arms are bent. He pushes his body forward until it is extended and then begins to push upward and backward until the original position is resumed. The shoulder should describe a complete circle. In the beginning, the vaulter does five repetitions.

The one-arm side push-up begins from a prone position. The vaulter's arms are in a reverse T position, and then following a rotating move from left to right and right to left are pushed up. One arm is extended and the other is flexed. Five of these for each side are adequate at the start. Running follows this exercise and consists of three laps around the gymnasium perimeter with forward rolls.

The leg throw is the first of the partner exercises. A vaulter lies in a supine position with his legs together and fully extended. His partner stands with his feet straddling the vaulter's head. The vaulter raises his legs with the knees extended toward his partner. As the legs move up toward the partner, he pushes them at the area of the ankles back toward the starting position. This exercises is continued for 20 repetitions. The fireman's carry with bending action is next as the partner is placed on the shoulders of the vaulter who does knee bends.

For the leg press exercise the vaulter lies on his back with his arms at his side for balance. His hands are crossed on his chest. The partner stands facing the vaulter with the palms of his hands on the vaulter's feet. Resistance is applied on the bottom of the feet as the vaulter extends his legs to full extension. This exercise is done alternately, first ten times for each leg and then together ten times.

When he is preparing to do the shoulder strength and flexibilty exercise, the vaulter extends his arms at shoulder height to each side as he is standing. His partner stands behind him with his back to the vaulter's back. Their hands are interlocked with fingers not interlocking. Both men apply resistance by bringing the arms forward.

To conclude Monday's workout, which is the first day of each week's program, the vaulter runs three more time around the gymnasium doing the forward rolls.

On Wednesday, which is the next workout day, the same exercises are repeated, with the exception of the partner exercise. In place of these drills, the medicine ball is used. A 10- to 14-pound medicine ball is used for the

Pole vaulting requires a very high level of muscular fitness.

wrists strength exercise. The vaulter assumes a standing position and places the ball in front of his chest. Holding the ball with his hands placed on each side, he rotates his hands, with the thumbs leading as far as possible, and returns them to their original position. Twenty of these exercises should be done in a set.

For the shoulder strength exercise the vaulter holds the ball out in front with his arms extended. He moves the ball above his head with the arms remaining in an extended position. Ten of these should be done in a set.

The waist and hip exercise is next. Instruct the vaulter to assume a straddle position with his trunk flexed. The ball is held 5 to 10 inches above the floor. Then the vaulter swings the ball to the left and then to the right to shoulder height. As the ball is swung to the left again, it continues to a complete arc and the vaulter extends his body upward. Twenty of these should be done in one set.

Lying in a supine position, the vaulter places his left hand on the floor with the palm up and extended above his head. The ball is placed on the vaulter's hand and his right hand is placed on top of the ball. His hips and shoulders are kept flat, allowing no lift. The ball is lifted with a five-count to the opposite side so that the vaulter's right hand is under the ball and his left hand is on top. The hand is not allowed to touch the floor. Return with the same count. After five repetitions, the hand position is changed.

Next, the vaulter assumes a prone position. He places the ball in front with his arms extended. His hands are placed on each side of the ball. The ball is raised off the floor and the vaulter's back is arched as far as possible. At the peak position the ball is held for a five-count.

From a sitting position, with his legs extended and the ball between his feet, the vaulter executes the abdominal exercise. He extends his arms and places them slightly behind his body. Then he lifts the ball with the ankles. This is a five-count exercise.

For the leg-strengthening exercise the vaulter assumes a standing position with his drive leg back and lead leg forward. His lead leg is flexed and the drive leg is slightly flexed. The ball is placed above his head. His hips are moved forward to extend the drive leg completely. This exercise is done ten times. Then the ball is placed in front and held on each side with the hands. This exercise is done ten times and concludes Wednesday's exercises.

Friday's workout is the same as Monday's and Wednesday's, except apparatus is used in place of partner exercises.

Next on the program are bar pullups, two sets of five repetitions. Then the big log circle is done on the high or uneven bar. The stall bar which is stationary against the wall can also be used. This exercise is performed by hanging on the bar and pulling the body up with the elbows bent. The vaulter's knees are brought toward his trunk with the knees bent slightly. His legs are swung in a circular motion with the hips up. Six of these exercises should be done at the start of the program.

For the hip circle on the rings, the rings are set at shoulder height. The vaulter pulls up on the right with his hands until his feet leave the floor and can be rotated in a small circle. His legs are kept together and his eyes are fixed on an object straight ahead. The size of the circle is increased until the arms are fully extended. About ten of these should be done.

Have the vaulter lie down on the horse in a prone position with his hips at the edge and his trunk extended over the end. A partner holds his legs, the vaulter bends down as far as possible, and then lifts up as far as possible, arching his back. His hands are clasped and placed behind his head. Ten repetitions are advised to complete this exercise.

The last exercise is the bent arm round-off with a push on the horse. With a running approach the vaulter takes off on one foot and does a handstand. He pushes upward, rotates his body, and lands on the opposite side. Do five to ten of these. As a safety measure, a spotter should be placed in front of the horse until the athlete has become proficient at this exercise. This exercise concludes Friday's exercises.

A major concern of all coaches should be that their athletes progress physically to meet the competition.

These exercises are supplemented with workouts on the track. The major concern is to have the vaulter progress physically to meet the competition. Our vaulters work with the sprinters the first two weeks and continue throughout the season with the sprinters two days a week, Tuesday and Thursday. We realize that a vaulter must increase his initial take-off velocity by improving his running approach; therefore, sprint work is essential. To accomplish form, we work on techniques three days a week and take films early in the season to use as a guide for improvement. Since our techniques are essentially the same as those used by most coaches in training vaulters, we feel our advantage has come as a result of the gymnastics program that has been used the last two years.

ABOUT THE EDITOR

Currently the head track and field coach at the University of Florida, John Randolph has compiled a varied and outstanding record of success on the collegiate, national, and international levels. From 1976-1980, he was the chairman of the NCAA Track and Field Rules Committee. He has also served as a member of both the AAU and Olympic Development Committees. Currently, he is the chairman of the Men's Olympic Development Committee for the preparation period leading up to the Los Angeles Olympic Games. In 1977 he was head coach of the USA National Junior Team that scored impressive wins over USSR in both men's and women's competition, and in 1978 he coached the Eastern Team in the first National Sports Festival in Colorado Springs.

From 1976 until his appointment at Florida, Randolph was head coach at the U.S. Military Academy where his West Point teams posted an excellent 54-4-1 record, including two unbeaten indoor teams. He coached seven all-Americans and developed numerous Academy record holders. In 1978 his entire cross country team qualified for the NCAA championship.

A 1964 graduate of William and Mary, Randolph returned to his alma mater in 1968 as an assistant coach while earning a master's degree in Educational Administration and Physical Education. The following year he was named head coach of the Tribe and proceeded to lead them to a record 52 championships in cross country, indoor and outdoor track in Southern Conference and Virginia Intercollegiate competition. In nine years his teams won eight Southern Conference cross country and indoor track titles, and seven outdoor crowns.

While at the Virginia school he coached 11 all-Americans, three NCAA individual champions (Juris Luzins and Reggie Clark in the 800; Howell Michael in the 1500), and four USA National Team members. He was named Southern Conference Coach-of-the-Year in cross country, indoor and outdoor track in both 1975 and 1976, and was named NCAA District 3 Southeast Coach-of-the-Year in 1972 for indoor track and 1973 for cross country.

Randolph earned two letters in cross country and six in track while an undergraduate at William and Mary, competing in the 220, 440, and 880. He won the Southern Conference in the 440 and was a member of the mile relay team, and was named the school's "Outstanding Senior Athlete" upon graduation.